Solut

for

PROBABILITY FOR RISK MANAGEMENT

Second Edition

by

Donald G. Stewart, Ph.D.

and

Matthew J. Hassett, ASA, Ph.D.

ACTEX Publications
Winsted, Connecticut

Requests for permission should be addressed to
    ACTEX Publications
    P.O. Box 974
    Winsted, CT 06098

Manufactured in the United States of America

10 9 8 7 6 5 4 3 2 1

ISBN: 978-1-56698-583-3
ISBN: 1-56698-548-X

CONTENTS

INTRODUCTORY NOTE

This solutions manual complements a study of probability theory, based on the second edition of the textbook *Probability for Risk Management*, by Matthew Hassett and Donald Stewart.

The solutions given here for basic problems are brief, and are intended to give an outline of how to proceed. If the reader understands the examples in the text, these solutions should be adequate. The solutions to the sample exam questions are more detailed.

In most cases there will be more than one way to work a problem. The reader may expect to encounter solutions which differ from those given here.

CHAPTER 2

2-1.   The red suits are hearts (H) and diamonds (D), and the face cards kings (K), queens (Q) and jacks (J). Thus the outcomes are KH, QH, JH, KD, QD and JD.

2-2.   (a) The loss can be any positive rational number.

(b) The loss is any rational number in (1,000, 1,000,000).

2-3.   (a) *S* consists of the positive integers from 1 to 25.

(b) *E* consists of the odd integers from 1 to 25.

2-4.   *S* consists of all ordered pairs (r, g) where $r = 1, 2, 3, 4, 5,$ or 6 and $g = 1, 2, 3, 4, 5,$ or 6.

2-5.   Count the number of ordered pairs with the desired sum in the list in the answer For Exercise 2-4. For example, the only two pairs which sum to 11 are $(5, 6)$ and $(6, 5)$, so the answer to part (c) is 2.

2-6.   *S* consist of all sequences *xyz* where each of *x*, *y* and *z* is either *B* or *G*.

2-7.   The outcomes in ~*E* are the even (not odd) integers between 1 and 25.

2-8.   The outcomes in $A \cap B$ are the club face cards.

2-9. $A \cup B$ is all rational numbers in (1,000, 500,000).
        $A \cap B$ is all rational numbers in (50,000, 100,000).

2-10. $A \cap B$ requires an outcome where the coin shows a head and the
        number on the die is greater than 2. It consists of the ordered
        pairs $(H,3)$, $(H,4)$, $(H,5)$, and $(H,6)$.

2-11. $E = \{(1,5),(2,4),(3,3),(4,2),(5,1)\}$
        $F = \{(1,1),(2,2),(3,3),(4,4),(5,5),(6,6)\}$
        $E \cup F = \{(1,5),(2,4),(3,3),(4,2),(5,1),(1,1),(2,2),(4,4),(5,5),(6,6)\}$
        $E \cap F = \{(3,3)\}$

2-12. $E = \{GGG, GGB, GBG, GBB\}$
        $F = \{GBG, GBB, BBG, BBB\}$
        $E \cup F = \{GGG, GGB, GBG, GBB, BBG, BBB\}$
        $E \cap F = \{GBG, GBB\}$

2-13.   To verify (2.1) draw a Venn diagram for $A \cap (B \cup C)$ and a
        second one showing $(A \cap B)$ and $(A \cap C)$ and observe that the
        first is the union of the second and the third.

$A \cap (B \cup C)$ $(A \cap B) \cup (A \cap C)$

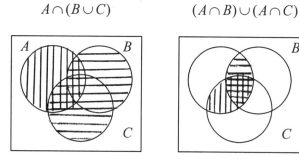

To verify (2.2) draw a Venn diagram for $A \cup (B \cap C)$ and a second one showing $(A \cup B)$ and $(A \cup C)$, and observe that first is the intersection of the second and the third.

$$A \cup (B \cap C) \qquad\qquad (A \cup B) \cap (A \cup C)$$

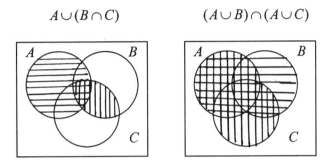

2-14.   To verify (2.3) draw a Venn diagram for $\sim (A \cup B)$ and a second one showing $\sim A$ and $\sim B$, and verify that the first is the intersection of the second and the third.

$$\sim (A \cup B) \qquad\qquad \sim A \cap \sim B$$

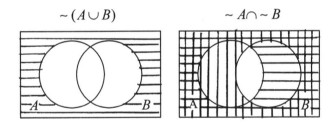

To verify (2.4) draw a Venn diagram for $\sim (A \cap B)$ and a second one showing $\sim A$ and $\sim B$, and verify that the first is the union of the second and the third.

$$\sim (A \cap B) \qquad\qquad \sim A \cup \sim B$$

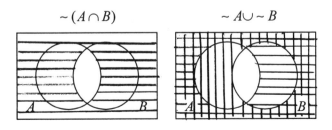

2-15.   See verbal statements in Answers to the Exercises.

2-16.   Let H be the set of those with health insurance and L be the set of those with life insurance. Then $(L \cup H) = 38 + 29 - 21 = 46$.

2-17.   Let L be the set of those with the company more than 10 years and D be the set of those with college degrees. The given data can be used to fill in the Venn diagram below. Then $n(L \cup D) = 134 - 23 = 111$. Then $n(D) = n(L \cup D) - 19 = 111 - 19 = 92$.

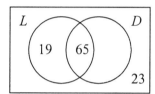

2-18   Let S be the set of those who own stocks and B be the set of those who own bonds. So $n(S \cap B) = 67 + 52 - 94 = 25$.

2-19.   The given data can be used to fill in the Venn diagram below. The number of students taking exactly one of these courses is $54 + 38 = 92$.

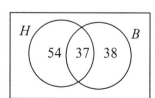

2-20.   Using the given information we get the following Venn diagram.

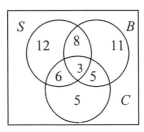

The total number of clients is 61.

2-21.   Using the given information we get the following Venn diagram.

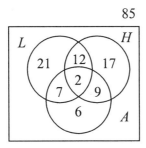

(a) The number with no policies is $85 - 74 = 11$.
(b) The number with only health policies is 17.
(c) The number with exactly one policy is $21 + 17 + 6 = 44$.
(d) The number with life or health but not auto is
      $21 + 12 + 17 = 50$.

2-22.   Number of outcomes is $2 \cdot 6 = 12$.

2-23.   Number of ways to select car is $4 \cdot 15 \cdot 6 = 360$.

2-24.   Number of ways to select classes is $7 \cdot 8 \cdot 4 \cdot 7 = 1568$.

2-25.   Number of outcomes is $26 \cdot 2 + 26 \cdot 6 = 208$.

2-26.   Each subset corresponds with exactly one sequence. For example the subset $\{x_1, x_2\}$ corresponds with the sequence $(1,1,0,0,...,0)$. There are 2^n sequences, so there are 2^n subsets.

2-27.   If repetitions are allowed, the number of words is $6^4 = 1296$.

   If repetitions are not allowed, the number is $P(6,4) = 360$.

2-28.   If repetitions are allowed there are $8 \cdot 10^6$ possible numbers. If repetitions are not allowed there are

$$8 \cdot 9 \cdot 8 \cdot 7 \cdot 6 \cdot 5 \cdot 4 = 483,840$$

   numbers.

2-29.   The number of seating arrangements (in order) is

$$P(12,7) = 3,991,680.$$

2-30.   The number of rankings (in order) is $P(10,4) = 5040$.

2-31.   The number of ways to fill the offices is $P(30,3) = 24,360$.

2-32.   The number of seating arrangements is $P(4,4)P(6,6) = 17,280$. (Arrange the left-handers in the first 4 seats, and then arrange the right-handers in the remaining 6 seats.)

2-33.   First choose a pair of adjacent seats, which can be done in 7 ways, and the two people can be seated in those seats in 2 ways. Then arrange the 6 remaining people in remaining 6 chairs. This can be done in 6! ways, so the number of seating arrangements is $7 \cdot 2 \cdot 6! = 10,080$.

2-34.   The number of possible committees is $C(30,3) = 4060$. (Order is irrelevant.)

2-35.   The number of hands is $C(52,5) = 2,598,960$. (Order is irrelevant.)

2-36.   (a) Number of hands with all hearts is $C(13,5) = 1287$.

   (b) Number of hands with all same suit is $4C(13,5) = 5148$. (Choose one of the 4 suits and then choose 5 cards.)

   (c) Number of hands with (AAKKJ) is $C(4,2)C(4.2) \cdot 4 = 144$. (Choose 2 aces and then 2 kings and then 1 jack.)

2-37.   Number of ways to pick cast is $C(15,4)C(13,5) = 1,756,755$. (Choose 4 boys and then 5 girls.)

2-38.   Number of ways to select balls is $C(55,5) \cdot 42 = 146,107,962$.

2-39.   Number of distinguishable arrangements of MISSISSIPPI is $\frac{11!}{4!4!2!} = 34,650$. (There are 11 slots to fill with the 11 letters. First select 4 slots for the 4 I's, and then 4 slots for the 4 S's, and 2 slots for the 2 P's, leaving one slot left for the M.)

2-40.   Number of ways to assign the actuaries is $\frac{12!}{5!3!4!} = 27,720$, since this constitutes a partition of the group.

2-41.   Number of ways to assign the analysts is $9!/(3!)^3 = 1680,$ since this constitutes a partition of the group.

2-42.   In this case the 3 teams are not distinguishable by task. If the 9 analysts are divided into 3 three-man teams, A, B and C, and have distinguishable tasks, these teams can be assigned to the 3 tasks in $3! = 6$ ways. But if the tasks are all the same, those 6 partitions constitute a single division into teams. Hence the divisions into teams is the number of partitions divided by 6 which is $\frac{1680}{6} = 280.$

2-43. $(2s-t)^4 = (2s)^4 + 4(2s)^3(-t) + 6(2s)^2(-t)^2 + 4(2s)(-t)^3 + (-t)^4$

2-44.   Term is $C(8,3)(2u)^5(-3v)^3$, and coefficient is $-48,384.$

2-45.   An $x^{n-k}y^k$ is obtained by selecting k of the $(x+y)$ factors from which to take y and taking x from the remaining $n-k$ factors. This can be done in $C(n,k)$ ways.

2-46.   The number of subsets of size k from a set of size n is $C(n,k)$. Then $2^n = (1+1)^n = \Sigma C(n,k)$ equals the total number of subsets.

2-47.   This is a standard counting problem from finite mathematics courses. It is usually visualized with a Venn diagram. Let Y denote the event that the policyholder is young, M the event that he is male and H the event that the policy holder is married. We need the count from the shaded region. The intersection of all three circles contains the 600 young married males, and $n(Y \cap H \cap M) = 600.$ Since there are 1320 young males, $n(Y \cap M) = 1320$ and the remaining segment of $Y \cap M$ will contain 720 young single males. Similarly, since there are 1400 young married persons, $n(Y \cap H) = 1400$ and the remaining segment of $Y \cap M$ will contain 800 young married females. Then the shaded region contains $3000 - (800+600+720) = 880$ young single females.

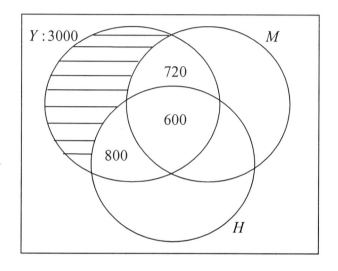

CHAPTER 3

3-1.   There are 8 total outcomes, 3 of which give 2 heads and 1 tail, HHT, HTH or THH. Hence P(2 heads and 1 tail) $= \frac{3}{8}$.

3-2. $P(\text{at least 1 head}) = 1 - P(\text{no heads}) = 1 - \frac{1}{8} = \frac{7}{8}$

3-3.   (a) $P(\text{ball is red}) = \frac{3}{16}$

       (b) $P(\text{ball is not green}) = P(\text{ball is red or blue}) = \frac{6+3}{16} = \frac{9}{16}$

3-4.   Number of employees with degree in either mathematics or economics is $21 + 33 - 7 = 47$. The probability that the person chosen has one of these is $\frac{47}{68}$.

3-5.   There are 36 outcomes, of which 6 give a 7, 2 an 11, and 6 give a number less that 5.

       (a) $P(7) = \frac{6}{36}$

       (b) $P(11) = \frac{2}{36}$

       (c) $P(\text{less than 5}) = \frac{6}{36}$

3-6.   Number of clients with either life or auto insurance is $45 + 32 - 16 = 61$. The probability a client has neither is $\frac{17}{78}$.

3-7.   (a) $P(\text{all 3 red}) = \dfrac{C(4,3)}{C(10,3)} = \dfrac{4}{120} = \dfrac{1}{30}$

      (b) $P(\text{1 red and 2 green}) = \dfrac{C(4,1)C(6,2)}{120} = \dfrac{60}{120} = \dfrac{1}{2}$

      (c) $P(\text{all red or all green}) = \dfrac{C(4,3)+C(6,3)}{120} = \dfrac{24}{120} = \dfrac{1}{5}$

3-8.   (a) $P(\text{all 4 good}) \dfrac{C(35,4)}{C(40,4)} = \dfrac{52,360}{91,390} = .5279$ $0,5724$

      (b) $P(\text{2 good and 2 defective}) = \dfrac{C(35,2)C(5,2)}{C(40,4)}$

$$= \dfrac{5,950}{91,390} = .0651$$

3-9.   Total seating arrangements is $10! = 3,628,800$. There are two choices, M or W, for the first chair. This determines the 5 chairs for the 5 men and the 5 chairs for the 5 women. The number of seating arrangements alternating men and women is $2(5!)(5!) = 28,800$. The probability is .0079.

3-10.   P(at least 2 born on same date)
$$= 1 - P(\text{all born on different days})$$
$$= 1 - \dfrac{P(31,8)}{31^8} = .6271$$

3-11.   P(at least 2 born on same day of week)
$$= 1 - P(\text{all born on different days})$$
$$= 1 - \dfrac{P(7,4)}{7^4} = .6501$$

3-12.   P(balls of both colors) $= 1 - P(\text{all red or all blue})$
$$= 1 - \dfrac{C(5,4)+C(6,4)}{C(11,4)}$$
$$= 1 - \dfrac{20}{330} = \dfrac{31}{33}$$

3-13.   Number of hands is 2,598,960 (Exercise 2-35). Number of ways to pick the 2 ranks is $P(13,2)$. Number of full houses is $P(13,2)C(4,3)C(4,2) = 3744$, so $P(\text{full house}) = .0014$.

3-14.   Number of ways to pick 2 suits for pairs is $C(13,2)$. (Order doesn't matter here.) Number of hands is
$C(13.2)C(4,2)C(4,2)\cdot 44 = 123,552$, so $P(\text{two pair}) = .0475$.

3-15.   (a) $P(7) = \frac{1}{6}$, $P(\sim 7) = \frac{5}{6}$. Odds for a 7 are 1:5.

      (b) $P(11) = \frac{1}{18}$, $P(\sim 11) = \frac{17}{18}$. Odds against an 11 are 17:1.

3-16.   If the odds against F are $a:b$, the odds for F are $b:a$, and
$$P(F) = \frac{b}{b+a}.$$

3-17. $E \cup \sim E = S$ and $E \cap \sim E = \emptyset$, so $P(E) + P(\sim E) = P(S) = 1$.

3-18. $A = (A \cap B) \cup (A \cap \sim B)$ and $B = (B \cap A) \cup (B \cap \sim A)$, so
$(A \cup B) = (A \cap \sim B) \cup (A \cap B) \cup (B \cap \sim A)$.

$$\begin{aligned}
P(A \cup B) &= P(A \cap \sim B) + P(A \cap B) + P(B \cap \sim A) \\
&= P\big((A \cap \sim B) + P(A \cap B) + P(B \cap \sim A)\big) \\
&\quad + \big[P(A \cap B) - P(A \cap B)\big] \\
&= P(A) + P(B) - P(A \cap B)
\end{aligned}$$

3-19. $P(\text{junior or senior}) = .244 + .215 = .459$

3-20. $P(\text{no claim}) = 1 - P(\text{liability or comprehensive})$
$$= 1 - (.22 + .37 - .13) = .54$$

3-21. (a) $P(C \text{ or better}) = .131 + .278 + .312 = .721$

(b) $P(D \text{ or } E) = .089 + .094 = .183$

3-22. $P(\text{flu shot or tuberculosis test})$
$$= 1 - .21 = .79$$
$$= P(\text{flu shot}) + P(\text{tuberculosis test}) - P(\text{both})$$
$$= .37 + .58 - P(\text{both}).$$

$P(\text{both}) = .95 - .79 = .16$

3-23. $P(A|C \text{ or better}) = \frac{.131}{.721} = .1817$

3-24. $P(\text{missed 1 day}|\text{missed work}) = \frac{.237}{.365} = .6493$

3-25. $P(\text{low claim}|\text{claim filed}) = \frac{.169}{.208} = .8125$

3-26. (a) $P(\text{both hearts}) = P(1^{\text{st}} \text{ heart})P(2^{\text{nd}} \text{ heart}|1^{\text{st}} \text{ heart})$
$$= \left(\tfrac{1}{4}\right)\left(\tfrac{12}{51}\right) = .0588$$
(b) $P(\text{neither a heart})$
$$= P(1^{\text{st}} \text{ not a heart})P(2^{\text{nd}} \text{ not a heart}|1^{\text{st}} \text{ not a heart})$$
$$= \left(\tfrac{3}{4}\right)\left(\tfrac{38}{51}\right) = .5588$$
(c) $P(\text{exactly one heart}) = 1 - .0588 - .5588 = .3824$

3-27. $P(\text{exactly 2 heads }|\text{at least 1 head}) = \left(\tfrac{3}{8}\right)\Big/\left(\tfrac{7}{8}\right) = \left(\tfrac{3}{7}\right)$

3-28. $P(\text{exactly 2 heads} \mid 1^{st} \text{ is a head})$

$$= \frac{P(\text{exactly 2 heads and } 1^{st} \text{ is a head})}{P(1^{st} \text{ is a head})}$$

$$= \left(\tfrac{2}{8}\right)/\left(\tfrac{4}{8}\right) = \tfrac{1}{2}$$

3-29. Let E be the event exactly 2 cards are hearts and F be the event all three are hearts. $E \cup F$ is the event at least 2 are hearts. Then $n(E) = C(13,2)(39) = 3042$ and $n(F) = C(13,3) = 286$, so

$P(E \mid E \cup F) = \frac{286}{286+3042} = .0859.$

3-30. Let E be the event the card is a spade. $P(A) = P(B) = P(C) = \tfrac{1}{2}$.

$$P(A \cap B) = P(A \cap C) = P(B \cap C) = P(S) = \tfrac{1}{4}$$
$$= P(A)P(B)$$
$$= P(A)P(C)$$
$$= P(B)P(C),$$

so each pair is independent.

$$P(A \cap B \cap C) = P(S) = \tfrac{1}{4} \neq P(A)P(B)P(C)$$

3-31. $P(A1 \cap A2) = \frac{4^2}{52^2}$, and $P(A2) = \frac{4}{52} = P(A1)$

$P(A2 \mid A1) = \frac{P(A1 \cap A2)}{P(A1)} = \frac{4}{52} = P(A2)$, so events are independent.

3-32. $P(A) = \tfrac{2}{3}$, $P(B) = \tfrac{1}{2}$ and $P(C) = \tfrac{1}{2}$.

$P(A \cap B) = \tfrac{1}{2} \neq P(A)P(B)$, so pair is dependent.

$P(A \cap C) = \tfrac{1}{3} = P(A)P(C)$, so pair is independent.

$P(B \cap C) = \tfrac{1}{3} \neq P(B)P(C)$, so pair is dependent.

3-33. $P(\text{color blind}) = \frac{9}{300}$, and $P(\text{color blind} | \text{male}) = \frac{7}{130}$.
       Male and color blind are dependent.

3-34. (a) $P(\text{pass both classes}) = (.75)(.84) = .63$

       (b) $P(\text{fail both classes}) = (.25)(.16) = .04$
            $P(\text{pass exactly one class}) = 1 - (.63 + .04) = .33$

3-35. $P(\text{none break down}) = .95^3 = .8574$

3-36. $P(\text{at least one fails}) = 1 - P(\text{neither fails}) = 1 - (.83)(.88) = .2696$

3-37. $P(E) = \frac{1}{2}$ and $P(F) = \frac{3}{8}$. $P(E \cap F) = \frac{1}{4}$. ($E \cap F = \{\text{HHT,HTH}\}$)
       $P(E \cap F) \neq P(E)P(F)$, so events are dependent.

3-38. (a) $P(\text{injury}) = (.6)(.35) + (.4)(.2) = .29$
       (b) $P(\text{assembly line worker} | \text{injury}) = \frac{.08}{.29} = .2759$

3-39. $P(\text{nickel}) = \left(\frac{1}{2}\right)\left(\frac{4}{15}\right) + \left(\frac{1}{2}\right)\left(\frac{1}{3}\right) = \frac{3}{10}$

       $P(\text{jar II} | \text{nickel}) = \left(\frac{1}{6}\right) / \left(\frac{3}{10}\right) = \frac{5}{9}$

3-40. $P(0 \text{ claims}) = (.6)(.8) + (.4)(.5) = .68$
       $P(2 \text{ claims}) = (.6)(.05) + (.4)(\underset{0.2}{.02}) = .11$

       (a) $P(\text{low risk} | 0 \text{ claims}) = \frac{.48}{.68} = .7059$
       (b) $P(\text{high risk} | 2 \text{ claims}) = \frac{.08}{.11} = .7273$

3-41. $P(\text{defective}) = (.4)(.01) + (.35)(.02) + (.25)(.04) = .021$

   $P(\text{machine A}|\text{defective}) = \frac{.004}{.021} = .1905$

3-42.   Define the events; D: has disease, $\sim D$: doesn't have disease, Y: tests positive, and N: tests negative.

   $P(Y) = (.2)(.95) + (.8)(.3) = .43$, and
   $P(N) = (.2)(.05) + (.8)(.7) = .57$

   (a) $P(\sim D|Y) = \frac{.24}{.43} = .5581$

   (b) $P(D|N) = \frac{.01}{.57} = .0175$

3-43.   Let A be event first card is a heart, and B that second is a heart.

   $P(A \cap B) = \left(\frac{1}{4}\right)\left(\frac{12}{51}\right)$, and $P(\sim A \cap B) = \left(\frac{3}{4}\right)\left(\frac{13}{51}\right)$.

   $P(\text{second card is a heart}) = \frac{12 + 39}{4 \cdot 51} = \frac{1}{4}$

3-44. $P(\text{severe injury}) = (.7)(.10) + (.3)(.15) = .115$

   $P(\text{plant A}|\text{severe injury}) = \frac{.07}{.115} = .6087$

3-45. $P(\text{injury}) = 1 - P(\text{no injury}) = 1 - \left[(.7)(.6) + (.3)(.5)\right] = .43$

   $P(\text{plant } B \text{ and minor injury}|\text{injury}) = \frac{(.3)(.35)}{.43} = .2442$

3- 46.   Let L denote the event that lab work results from the visit and S the event that the visit results in a visit to a specialist.

We are given that $P\left[\sim(L\cup S)\right] = .35 = 1-P\left[(L\cup S)\right]$. Thus $\Pr(L\cup S)=.65$. We are given $P(S)=.30$ and $P(L)=.40$. This enables us to find $\Pr(L\cap S)$, since

$$P(L\cup S) = .65 = P(L)+P(S)-P(L\cap S)$$
$$= .40+.30-P(L\cap S)$$

This gives us $\Pr(L\cap S)=.05$.

3-47.   The Venn diagram below is used to help in solving the problem

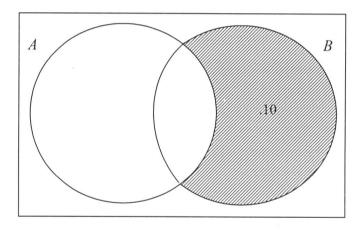

The area of the unshaded region represents $P[A\cup B']=.90$. Thus the area of the shaded region must be .10. The total area of the two circles represents $P(A\cup B)=.70$. Subtracting the area of the shaded region we get

$$P(A) = .70-.10 = .60.$$

3-48.   Let M denote the event that a customer insures more than one car and S denote the event that the customer insures a sports car. The required probability is   cle Morgan's laws (p. 19)

$$P(\sim M \cap \sim S) = P\left[\sim (M \cup S)\right] = 1 - P(M \cup S).$$

We will use a Venn diagram to visualize the problem. The required value is represented by the area outside of the two circles in the Venn diagram below. The first step in the solution is to use the given information that 15% of those who insure more than one car insure a sports car. This implies that $P(M \cap S) = .15(.64) = .096$ as indicated in the Venn diagram. Since we are given $P(M) = .64$, we see that the remaining area in the circle for M is $.64 - .096 = .544 = P(M \cap \sim S)$. Similarly we see that the remaining area in the circle for S is $.20 - .096 = .104 = P(\sim M \cap S)$. Adding the three separate areas inside the two circles we obtain

$$P(M \cup S) = .104 + .096 + .544 = .744.$$

$$P(\sim M \cap \sim S) = P\left[\sim (M \cup S)\right] = 1 - P(M \cup S) = .256$$

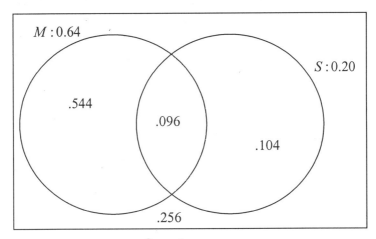

Or simply use formula

Pr (MUS) = Pr(M) + Pr(S) - Pr(M∩S)

= 0.64 + 0.20 - 0.096

= 0.744

3-49   Let P be the event that the patient visits a physical therapist and C the event that the patient visits a chiropractor. Since 12% of patients visit neither, we know that

$$.12 = P[\sim(P \cup C)] = 1 - P[P \cup C].$$

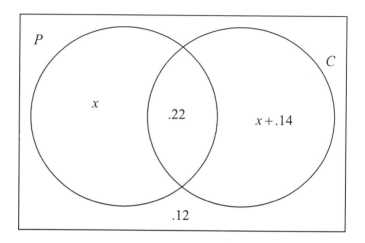

Thus $P(P \cup C) = .88$. We are also given that $P(P \cap C) = .22$. We use Venn diagram to organize the information.

Since we are not given $P(P)$, we denote $P(P \cap \sim C)$ by x, as indicated in the diagram. Then $P(P) = x + .22$. Since $P(C)$ exceeds $P(P)$ by .14, $P(C) = x + .22 + .14 = x + .36$. Now we know that $P(P \cup C) = .88 = x + .22 + x + .14 = 2x + .36$, which gives $x = .26$. Then $P(P) = x + .22 = .48$.

3-50.   Let *G* be the event that a group member watched gymnastics, *S* the event that she watched soccer and *B* the event that she watched baseball.

We need to find $P\left[\sim(G\cup B\cup S)\right]$. We will first use the Venn diagram to find $P(G\cup S\cup B)$, represented by the area inside of the three circles in the Venn diagram. We work from the inside out , starting with $P(G\cap S\cap B)=.08$. The results are

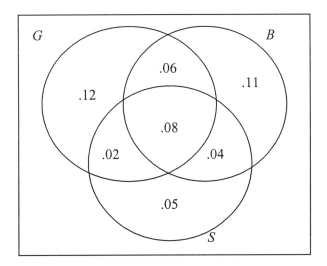

Thus

$$P(G\cup S\cup B) \;=\; .08+.06+.04+.02+.12+.11+.05 \;=\; .48$$

and

$$P\left[\sim(G\cup B\cup S)\right] \;=\; 1-.48 \;=\; .52\,.$$

3-51.   Let C be the event that an owner purchases collision insurance
        and D be the event that an owner purchases disability insurance.
        We need to find

$$P[\sim(C\cup D)] = 1 - P(C\cup D).$$

We review what the assumptions (i)-(iii) tell us.

(i) $P(C) = 2P(D)$.
(ii) $P(C\cap D) = P(C)P(D)$ by independence.
(iii) $P(C\cap D) = .15$

It follows that

$$.15 = P(C\cap D) = P(C)P(D) = 2P(D)^2$$
$$P(D)^2 = .075 \rightarrow P(D) = \sqrt{.075}$$
$$P(C) = 2P(D) = 2\sqrt{.075}$$

$$P(C\cup D) = P(C) + P(D) - P(C\cap D)$$
$$= 2\sqrt{.075} + \sqrt{.075} - .15 = .67$$

$$P[\sim(C\cup D)] = 1 - P(C\cup D) = 1 - .67 = .33$$

3-52.   Let E denote the event that a claim includes emergency room
        charges and O denote the event that a claim includes operating
        room charges. We need to find $P(O)$. We will use a Venn
        Diagram to assist with visualizing the problem. We are given
        that $P(E\cup O) = .85$. Thus $P[\sim(E\cup O)] = .15$.

We are also given that $P(\sim E) = .25$. The area representing
$P(\sim E)$ consists of the area outside the two circles and the
segment of the O circle which does not intersect the E circle –
i.e., $\sim E = \sim(E\cup O)\cup(\sim E\cap O)$. Thus the area of the segment
of the O circle which does not intersect the E circle is .10.

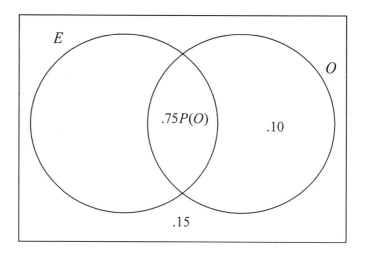

We are also given that E and O are independent. Thus
$$P(E \cap O) = P(E)P(O) = .75P(O).$$

It follows that

$$P(O) = .75P(O) + .10 \rightarrow P(O) = .40.$$

3-53. We are asked to find

$$P(N \geq 1 \mid N \leq 4) = \frac{P(N \geq 1 \,\&\, N \leq 4)}{P(N \leq 4)} = \frac{P(1 \leq N \leq 4)}{P(N \leq 4)}.$$

Below we tabulate the values of $P[N = n]$ for $0 \leq n \leq 4$.

n	0	1	2	3	4
$P[N = n]$	1/2	1/6	1/12	1/20	1/30

Thus

$$P(N \leq 4) = \tfrac{1}{2} + \tfrac{1}{6} + \tfrac{1}{12} + \tfrac{1}{20} + \tfrac{1}{30} = \tfrac{50}{60} = \tfrac{5}{6}$$

$$P(1 \leq N \leq 4) = \tfrac{1}{6} + \tfrac{1}{12} + \tfrac{1}{20} + \tfrac{1}{30} = \tfrac{20}{60} = \tfrac{1}{3}$$

$$P(N \geq 1 \mid N \leq 4) = \frac{P(1 \leq N \leq 4)}{P(N \leq 4)} = \frac{(1/3)}{(5/6)} = \tfrac{2}{5}$$

3-54.   Let A denote the event that a man in the study had at least one
        parent with heart disease and H the event that a man in the study
        died of causes related to heart disease. We are asked to find
        $P(H \mid \sim A)$. Since we are given count information, we will use
        the identity

$$P(H \mid \sim A) = \frac{n(H \cap \sim A)}{n(\sim A)}.$$

We are given that $n(A) = 312$, so $n(\sim A) = 937 - 312 = 625$, We
will use the Venn diagram that follows to find $n(H \cap \sim A) = 108$.
We are given that $n(A \cap H) = 102$. Since $n(H) = 210$, the
remainder of H contains 108 men –i.e., $n(H \cap \sim A) = 108$. Thus

$$P(H \mid \sim A) = \frac{n(H \cap \sim A)}{n(\sim A)} = \frac{108}{625} = .173$$

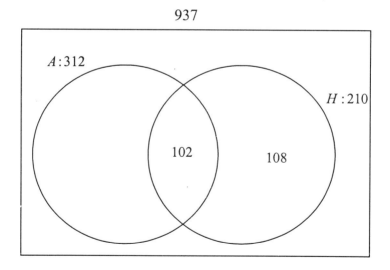

3-55. Denote the first and second urns by A and B respectively, and let x be the unknown number of blue balls in urn B. The next table summarizes the situation.

Urn	Red Balls	Blue Balls	Total Balls
A	4	6	10
B	16	x	$16+x$

Denote the event that a ball drawn from urn A is red (blue) by $R_A (B_A)$. Denote the event that a ball drawn from urn B is red (blue) by $R_B (B_B)$. The probability that both balls are the same color is

$$P(R_A \cap R_B) + P(B_A \cap B_B) = .4\left(\frac{16}{16+x}\right) + .6\left(\frac{x}{16+x}\right)$$
$$= \frac{6.4 + .6x}{16+x}$$

Note that we used the independence of the picks from the two urns to calculate each of the two probabilities using the multiplication rule.

The probability that both balls are the same color is .44. Thus

$$\frac{6.4 + .6x}{16+x} = .44$$
$$6.4 + .6x = .44(16) + .44x$$
$$.16x = .64 \rightarrow x = 4$$

3-56. We need to find

$$P(\sim A \cap \sim B \cap \sim C \mid \sim A) = \frac{P(\sim A \cap \sim B \cap \sim C)}{P(\sim A)}$$
$$= \frac{P[\sim (A \cup B \cup C)]}{P(\sim A)}$$

We will use a Venn diagram to keep score.

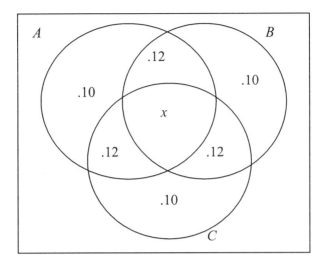

We are not given $P(A \cap B \cap C) = x$. We can fill in .12 in each of the areas representing exactly two risk factors and .10 in each of the areas representing exactly one risk factor. We are also given that the probability of a woman having all three risk factors given that she has A and B is 1/3. This gives us an equation to solve for x.

$$P(A \cap B \cap C \,|\, A \cap B) = \frac{P(A \cap B \cap C)}{P(A \cap B)} = \frac{1}{3}$$

From the Venn diagram

$$P(A \cap B \cap C) = x$$
$$P(A \cap B) = x + .12$$

Thus

$$\frac{x}{x + .12} = \frac{1}{3} \quad \rightarrow \quad x = .06$$

From the Venn diagram

$$P(A) = .06 + .12 + .12 + .10 = .40 \quad \rightarrow \quad P(\sim A) = .60$$

$$P(A \cup B \cup C) = .06 + 3(.12) + 3(.10) = .72$$

$$P[\sim (A \cup B \cup C)] = 1 - .72 = .28$$

Finally

$$P(\sim A \cap \sim B \cap \sim C \mid \sim A) = \frac{P[\sim (A \cup B \cup C)]}{P(\sim A)}$$

$$= \frac{.28}{.60} = .467$$

3-57.   We will use a Venn diagram to keep score.

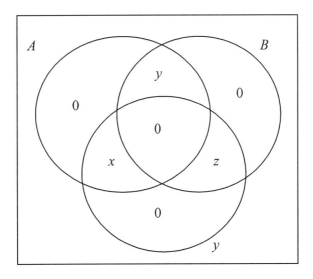

The regions representing exactly one and exactly three coverages have probability 0. The separate regions representing exactly two coverages have unknown probabilities x, y and z. We need to find $P[\sim (A \cup B \cup C)] = 1 - (x+y+z)$.

$$P(A) = x + y + 0 = \frac{1}{4}$$

$$P(B) = 0 + y + z = \frac{1}{3}$$

$$P(c) = x + 0 + z = \frac{5}{12}$$

The solution to the above system is $x = \frac{2}{12}, y = \frac{1}{12}, z = \frac{3}{12}$. Thus

$$P\left[\sim(A \cup B \cup C)\right] = 1 - (x + y + z) = 1 - \frac{6}{12} = \frac{1}{2}$$

3-58   Let A be the event that the policyholder has an auto policy and H be the event that she has a homeowners policy. Note that the following three events include all policyholders and are mutually exclusive:

$X_1 = A \cap H$:   The policyholder has both.
$X_2 = A \cap \sim H$:   The policyholder has auto only.
$X_3 = \sim A \cap H$:   The policyholder has homeowners only

These three events are a partition of the sample space.

We will use a Venn diagram to display the probabilities of the three events above.

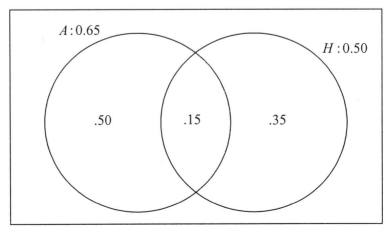

Now we know

$P(A \cap H) = .15 = \text{Pr[The policyholder has both.]}$
$P(A \cap \sim H) = .50 = \text{Pr[The policyholder has auto only]}$
$P(\sim A \cap H) = .35 = \text{Pr[The policyholder has homeowners only]}$

The problem gives conditional probabilities for renewal of at least one policy next year. We display the probabilities needed to solve the problem in a partial tree diagram.

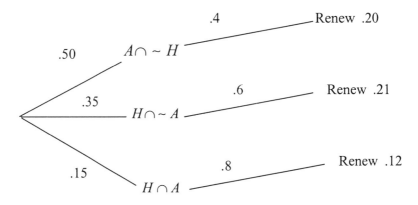

Recall that the events at the end of the first branch of the tree are a decomposition of the sample space. By the law of total probability,

$$P(\text{Renew}) = P(X_1 \cap \text{Renew})$$
$$+ P(X_2 \cap \text{Renew})$$
$$+ P(X_3 \cap \text{Renew})$$
$$= .20 + .21 + .12 = .53$$

3-59.   Let D be the event that a person has the disease and T the event
        that the test indicates the presence of the disease. We need to
        find $P(D|T)$. This is Bayes theorem problem. The tree diagram
        is

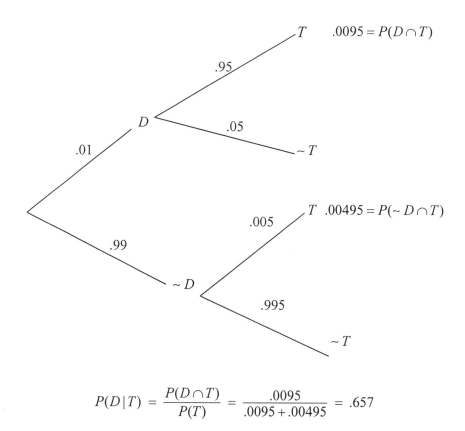

$$P(D|T) = \frac{P(D \cap T)}{P(T)} = \frac{.0095}{.0095 + .00495} = .657$$

3-60.   Let S, P and U denote the events that a policyholder is standard, preferred or ultra-preferred respectively. Let D denote the event that the policyholder dies. We are asked to find $P(U \mid D)$. This is a Bayes theorem problem. The partial tree is given below.

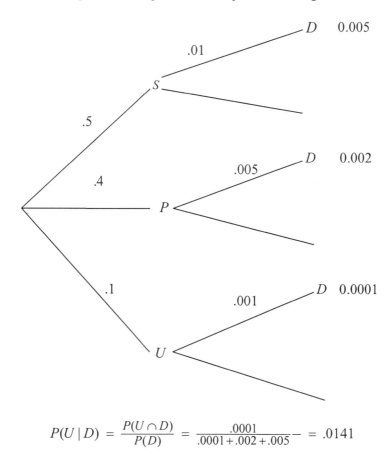

$$P(U \mid D) = \frac{P(U \cap D)}{P(D)} = \frac{.0001}{.0001 + .002 + .005} = .0141$$

3-61.   Let *C*, *SR* and *ST* denote the events that a patient was classified
         as critical, serious or stable respectively. Let *D* be the event that
         the patient dies. We need to find $P(SR \,|\sim D)$. This is a Bayes
         theorem problem. The tree diagram is below.

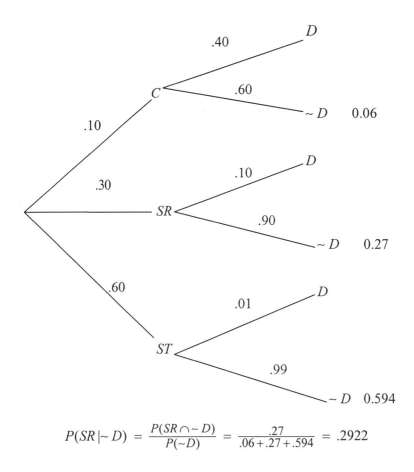

$$P(SR \,|\sim D) = \frac{P(SR \cap \sim D)}{P(\sim D)} = \frac{.27}{.06 + .27 + .594} = .2922$$

3-62   Let T, Y, M and S denote the events that a driver is teen, young adult, midlife or senior. Let O be the event that the driver is involved in at least one collision. We need to fine $P(Y|O)$. This is a Bayes theorem problem. The partial tree is below.

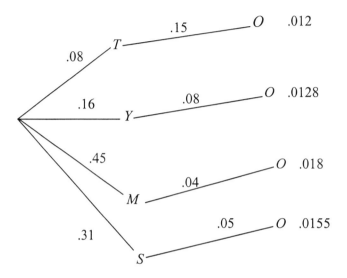

$$P(Y|O) = \frac{P(Y \cap O)}{P(O)} = \frac{.0128}{.012 + .0128 + .018 + .0155}$$

$$= .21955$$

3-63. Let C be the event that the randomly chosen male has a circulatory problem and S be the event that he is a smoker. We need to find $P(C|S)$. This is a Bayes theorem problem. The partial tree is below. Note that we do not know $x = P(S|\sim C)$ immediately, but we do know that $2x = P(S|C)$ since those who have a circulation problem are twice as likely to be smokers.

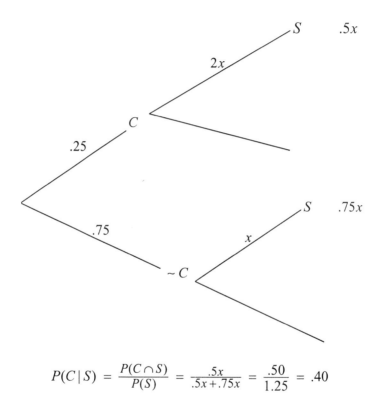

$$P(C|S) = \frac{P(C \cap S)}{P(S)} = \frac{.5x}{.5x + .75x} = \frac{.50}{1.25} = .40$$

3-64.   Let H, L and N denote the events that a person in the group is a heavy smoker, light smoker or nonsmoker respectively. Let D denote the event that the person dies. We need to find $P(H\,|\,D)$ This is a Bayes theorem problem. A partial tree is given below.

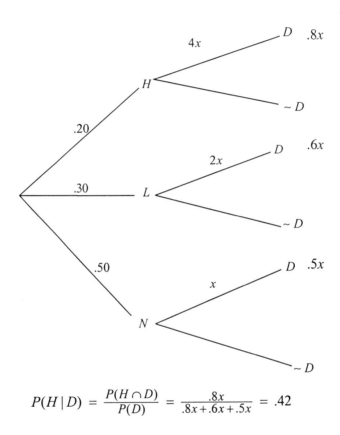

$$P(H\,|\,D) \;=\; \frac{P(H \cap D)}{P(D)} \;=\; \frac{.8x}{.8x+.6x+.5x} \;=\; .42$$

CHAPTER 4

4-1. Using the tree on page 26 we get the following table.

Number of heads (x)	0	1	2	3
Number of outcomes	1	3	3	1
$p(x)$	$\frac{1}{8}$	$\frac{3}{8}$	$\frac{3}{8}$	$\frac{1}{8}$

4-2. $P(X=0) = P(\text{first card is the ace}) = \frac{1}{10}$,

$P(X=1) = P(\text{second card is the ace} \mid \text{first was not the ace})$

$\cdot P(\text{first not the ace})$

$= \frac{9}{10} \cdot \frac{1}{9} = \frac{1}{10}$,

$P(X=2) = \frac{9}{10} \cdot \frac{8}{9} \cdot \frac{1}{8} = \frac{1}{10}$, etc.

4-3. $P(X=x) = \left(\frac{5}{6}\right)^x \left(\frac{1}{6}\right)$, $\quad x = 0,1,2,\ldots$

$F(x) = \frac{1}{6} + \frac{1}{6} \cdot \frac{5}{6} + \cdots + \left(\frac{1}{6}\right)\left(\frac{5}{6}\right)^x$

$= \left(\frac{1}{6}\right)\left(1 + \frac{5}{6} + \cdots + \left(\frac{5}{6}\right)^x\right) = \left(\frac{1}{6}\right)\dfrac{1-\left(\frac{5}{6}\right)^{x+1}}{1-\frac{5}{6}}$

$= 1 - \left(\frac{5}{6}\right)^{x+1}$, $\quad x = 0,1,2,\ldots$

4-4.

x	Number of Outcomes	$p(x)$	$F(x)$
2	1	1/36	1/36
3	2	2/36	3/36
4	3	3/36	6/36
5	4	4/36	10/36
6	5	5/36	15/36
7	6	6/36	21/36
8	5	5/36	26/36
9	4	4/36	30/36
10	3	3/36	33/36
11	2	2/36	35/36
12	1	1/36	36/36

4-5.
$$E(X) = \sum xp(x)$$
$$= \frac{2 + 3 \cdot 2 + 4 \cdot 3 + 5 \cdot 4 + 6 \cdot 5 + 7 \cdot 6 + 8 \cdot 5 + 9 \cdot 4 + 10 \cdot 3 + 11 \cdot 2 + 12}{36}$$
$$= 7$$

4-6.
$$E(X) = \frac{4 \cdot 15 + 3 \cdot 33 + 2 \cdot 51 + 6 \cdot 1 + 3 \cdot 0}{108} = 2.47$$

4-7.
$$E(X) = 0(.9929) + \$1000(.073) + \$10,000(.0041) = \$114$$
$$\text{Average cost per unit} = \frac{730(\$1000) + 41(\$10,000)}{10,000} = \$114$$

4-8.   If Y is the claim amount for one unit, then $X = 10Y + 50$.
From Exercise 4-7 we have $E(Y) = \$114$.
$$E(X) = E(10Y+50) = 10E(Y) + 50 = \$1140 + 50 = \$1190$$

4-9. $E(aX+b) = \sum (ax+b)p_Y(ax+b)$

$$= a\sum xp_X(x) + b\sum p_X(x) = aE(X) + b$$

4-10. $E(X) = \sum_{x=0}^{\infty} x\left(\frac{5}{6}\right)^x \left(\frac{1}{6}\right)$

$$= \left(\frac{5}{6}\right)\left(\frac{1}{6}\right)\sum_{x=1}^{\infty} x\left(\frac{5}{6}\right)^{x-1}$$

$$\frac{\left(\frac{5}{6}\right)\left(\frac{1}{6}\right)}{\left(1-\frac{5}{6}\right)^2} = \frac{\left(\frac{5}{6}\right)}{\left(\frac{1}{6}\right)} = 5$$

4-11.   Three outcomes yield 1 head and three outcomes yield 2 heads. Thus either 1 or 2 is a mode.

4-12. $V(X) = \sum (x-7)^2 p(x)$

$$= \frac{25+2(16)+3(9)+4(4)+5(1)+6(0)+5(1)+4(4)+3(9)+2(16)+25}{36}$$

$$= \frac{210}{36}$$

4-13. $V(X) = (10,000-114)^2(.0041) + (1000-114)^2(.073)$

$$+ (0-114)^2(.9229) = 470,004$$

For 5 units, $\sigma_{5X} = 5\sigma_X = 3427.84$

4-14.   If $Y = X+b, E(Y) = \mu_Y = E(X)+b = \mu_X + b.$

$$Y - \mu_Y = X+b-(\mu_X+b) = X - \mu_X$$

$$V(Y) = \Sigma(y-\mu_Y)^2 = \Sigma(x-\mu_X)^2 = V(X)$$

4-15.   (a) Lower bound is $1-\left(\frac{1}{2}\right)^2 = .75$.

(b) Two standard deviations equals $2(5.8333)^{1/2} = 4.8305$.

$$P(7-4.8305 < X < 7+4.8305) = P(3 \le X \le 11) = \frac{34}{36} = .9444$$

4-16. $\mu = \dfrac{0 \cdot 11,425 + 1 \cdot 3100 + 2 \cdot 385 + 3 \cdot 90}{15,000} = .276$

$\sigma^2 = \dfrac{11,425(0-.276)^2 + 3100(1-.276)^2 + 385(2-.276)^2 + 90(3-.276)^2}{15,000}$

$\quad = .0287157$

$\sigma \;\; = .53587$

4-17. $\bar{x} = \dfrac{0 \cdot 3 + 1 \cdot 5 + 2 \cdot 6 + 3 \cdot 9 + 4 \cdot 11 + 5 \cdot 7 + 6 \cdot 5 + 7 \cdot 3 + 8 \cdot 1}{50} = 3.64$

$s = \left(\dfrac{\sum f \cdot (n-3.64)^2}{49}\right)^{1/2} = 1.9667$

4-18.   First we need to find the mean and variance using the identities
$E(X) = \sum xp(x)$ and $V(X) = E(X^2) - E(X)^2 = E(X^2) - \mu^2$,
where $E(X^2) = \sum x^2 p(x)$. This is done most easily by adding
two more columns to the above table.

Claim Size	Probability	$xp(x)$	$x^2 p(x)$
20	0.15	3	60
30	0.10	3	90
40	0.05	2	80
50	0.20	10	500
60	0.10	6	360
70	0.10	7	490
80	0.30	24	1920
Total	1.00	55	3500

$$E(X) = \sum xp(x) = 55$$

$$\sigma^2 = V(X) = E(X^2) - \mu^2 = 3500 - 55^2 = 475$$

$$\sigma = \sqrt{475} = 21.8$$

A value is within one standard deviation of the mean if it is in the interval $[\mu - \sigma, \mu + \sigma]$, i.e., in the interval $[33.2, 76.8]$.

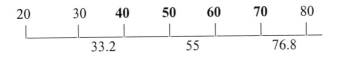

The values of x in this interval are 40, 50, 60 and 70. Thus the probability of being within one standard deviation of the mean is

$$p(40) + p(50) + p(60) + p(70) = .05 + .20 + .10 + .10 = .45.$$

4-19   Let X be the random variable for the present cost, and $Y = 1.2X$ the random variable for the cost after 20% inflation. We are asked to find $V(Y)$.

$$V(Y) = V(1.2X) = 1.2^2 V(X) = 1.44(260) = 374.4.$$

4-20   Note that the probability that an individual tourist will show up is .98. There are two key possibilities, which we summarize in the next table.

Number that show up	Probability	Revenue
21	$.98^{21} = .654$	$50(21) - 100 = 950$
< 21	$1 - .654 = .346$	$50(21) = 1050$

Thus the expected revenue is

$$.654(950) + .346(1050) = 984.6.$$

CHAPTER 5

5-1.   (a) $P(X=5) = C(10,5)\left(\frac{1}{2}\right)^5 \left(\frac{1}{2}\right)^5 = .2461 \quad \left(p=q=\frac{1}{2}\right)$

   (b) $P(X \geq 8) = C(10,8)\left(\frac{1}{2}\right)^{10} + C(10,9)\left(\frac{1}{2}\right)^{10} + C(10,10)\left(\frac{1}{2}\right)^{10}$
   $= .05469$

5-2.   (a) $P(X=2) = C(10,2)\left(\frac{1}{6}\right)^2 \left(\frac{5}{6}\right)^8 = .2907$

   (b) $P(X \geq 2) = 1 - P(X < 2) = 1 - \left[\left(\frac{5}{6}\right)^{10} + 10\left(\frac{1}{6}\right)\left(\frac{5}{6}\right)^9\right] = .5155$

5-3. $P(\text{three file claims}) = C(12,3)(.023)^3(.977)^9 = .00217$

5-4.   (a) $P(\text{exactly 2 defective}) = C(50,2)(.02)^2(.98)^{48} = .1858$
   (b) $\mu = 1000(.02) = 20; \quad \sigma^2 = 1000(.02)(.98) = 19.6$

5-5.   Let X be the random variable for the number of wins, and $Y = 100 - X$ be the random variable for the number of losses. The expected amount of gain $= E(10X) = 10(100)(.493) = 493$ and, the expected amount of loss $= E(10Y) = 10(100)(.507) = 507$. The expected end result is $493 - 507 = -14$ (a loss of \$14).

5-6.   (a) $P(4 \text{ have B+ blood}) = C(20,4)(.10)^4(.90)^{16} = .0898$
     (b) $P(\text{at most 3 have B+ blood})$
$$= (.90)^{20} + C(20,1)(.10)(.90)^{19}$$
$$+ C(20,2)(.10)^2(.90)^{18}$$
$$+ C(20,3)(.10)^3(.90)^{17} = .8670$$

5-7.   Let X be the number of pints of B+ blood donated.

$$E(X) = 50,000(.10) = 5000; \quad V(X) = 50,000(.10)(.90) = 4500$$

5-8.   (a) $P(2 \text{ aces}) = C(12,2)\left(\frac{1}{13}\right)^2\left(\frac{12}{13}\right)^{10} = .1754$

     (b) $P(3 \text{ hearts}) = C(12,3)\left(\frac{1}{4}\right)^3\left(\frac{3}{4}\right)^9 = .2581$

     (c) $P(\text{more than 1 heart}) = 1 - \left[\left(\frac{3}{4}\right)^{12} + 12\left(\frac{1}{4}\right)\left(\frac{3}{4}\right)^{11}\right] = .8416$

5-9. $P(\text{no more than 3}) = (.95)^{15} + C(15,1)(.05)(.95)^{14}$
$$+ C(15,2)(.05)^2(.95)^{13}$$
$$+ C(15,3)(.05)^3(.95)^{12}$$
$$= .9945$$

5-10. For a binomial random variable with $n = 2$ and $P(S) = p$ we
     have

k	0	1	2
$P(k)$	$(1-p)^2$	$2p(1-p)$	p^2

     (a) $E(X) = 0(1-p)^2 + 1(2p)(1-p) + 2p^2 = 2p$
     (b) $V(X) = (0-2p)^2(1-p)^2 + (1-2p)^2(2p)(1-p) + (2-2p)^2 p^2$
$$= 2p(1-p)\left[2p(1-p) + (1-2p)^2 + 2p(1-p)\right]$$
$$= 2p(1-p)$$

5-11. $P(2 \text{ aces}) = \dfrac{C(2,2)C(8,3)}{C(10,5)} = \dfrac{2}{9}$

5-12. $P(2 \text{ with AIDS}) = \dfrac{C(4,2)C(12,4)}{C(16,6)} = .3709$

5-13. (a) $P(4 \text{ of each}) = \dfrac{C(10,4)C(6,4)}{C(16,8)} = .2448$

(b) If X is number of left-handed batters, $E(X) = 8\left(\dfrac{6}{16}\right) = 3$

5-14. Let X be the number of Republicans on committee.

(a) $E(X) = 15\left(\dfrac{54}{100}\right) = 8.1$

(b) $V(X) = 15\left(\dfrac{54}{100}\right)\left(\dfrac{46}{100}\right)\left(\dfrac{85}{99}\right) = 3.199$

5-15. $E(X) = 13\left(\dfrac{1}{4}\right) = 3.25; \quad V(X) = 13\left(\dfrac{1}{4}\right)\left(\dfrac{3}{4}\right)\left(\dfrac{39}{51}\right) = 1.864$

5-16. (a) $P(X=1) = .6e^{-.6} = .3293$

(b) $P(X>1) = 1 - e^{-.6} - .6e^{-.6} = .1219$

5-17. (a) $P(X=0) = e^{-1.5} = .2231$

(b) $P(X=1) = 1.5e^{-1.5} = .3347$

(b) $P(X=2) = \dfrac{1.5^2 e^{-1.5}}{2} = .2510$

5-18. If X is the number of claims per year, $5000X$ is the claim amount.
$E(5000X) = 5000E(X) = 5000(.38) = 1900$

5-19.   (a) The rate of claims per policy per year is $\lambda = \dfrac{12,200}{50,000} = .244$.

    (b) $P(X=0 \text{ or } 1) = e^{-.244}(1+.244) = .9747$

    (c) $E(1000X) = 10000E(X) = 1000(.244) = 244$

5-20.   Let X and Y be the number of claims filed by two policyholders.

    (a) $P(X=1 \text{ and } Y=1) = (0.4e^{-.4})^2 = .0719$

    (b) $P(X=0 \text{ or } Y=0) = P(X=0) + P(Y=0) - P(X=0 \text{ and } Y=0)$
         $$= 2e^{-.4} - e^{-.8}$$
         $$= .8913.$$

5-21. $P(X=k-1) = \dfrac{k^{k-1}e^{-k}}{(k-1)!} = \dfrac{k}{k} \cdot \dfrac{k^{k-1}e^{-k}}{(k-1)!} = \dfrac{k^k e^{-k}}{k!} = P(X=k)$

    For

    $$n \geq k, P(X=n) = \frac{k^n e^{-k}}{n!}$$
    $$> \frac{k}{n+1} \cdot \frac{k^n e^{-k}}{n!}$$
    $$= \frac{k^{n+1}e^{-k}}{(n+1)!}$$
    $$= P(X=n+1)$$

    Hence for $n > k$, the probabilities get smaller as n gets larger.

    For $n < k-1, P(X=n) = \dfrac{k^n e^{-k}}{n!}$
    $$< \frac{k}{n+1} \cdot \frac{k^n e^{-k}}{n!}$$
    $$= \frac{k^{n+1}e^{-k}}{(n+1)!}$$
    $$= P(X = n+1)$$

    Hence for $n < k-1$, the probabilities get larger as n gets larger.
    Therefore the largest probability occurs when $n = k-1$ or k.

5-22. In Section 5.3.4 it was shown that $E(X) = \lambda$ for the Poisson random variable.

$$\begin{aligned}
V(X) &= E[(X-\lambda)^2] \\
&= E(X^2 - 2\lambda X + \lambda^2) \\
&= \sum_{k=0}^{\infty}(k^2 - 2\lambda k + \lambda^2)\frac{\lambda^k e^{-\lambda}}{k!} \\
&= \sum_{k=0}^{\infty} k^2 \frac{\lambda^k e^{-\lambda}}{k!} - 2\lambda \sum_{k=0}^{\infty} k \frac{\lambda^k e^{-\lambda}}{k!} + \lambda^2 \sum_{k=0}^{\infty} \frac{\lambda^k e^{-\lambda}}{k!}
\end{aligned}$$

The second term is $-2\lambda E(X) = -2\lambda^2$, and the last term is

$$\lambda^2 \sum p(x) = \lambda^2 (1).$$

$$\sum_{k=0}^{\infty} k^2 \frac{\lambda^k e^{-\lambda}}{k!} = \sum_{k=1}^{\infty} k \frac{\lambda^k e^{-\lambda}}{(k-1)!}$$

If we let $n = k - 1$, then $k = n + 1$ and this sum becomes

$$\sum_{n=0}^{\infty}(n+1)\frac{\lambda^{n+1} e^{-\lambda}}{n!} = \lambda \left(\sum_{n=0}^{\infty} n \frac{\lambda^n e^{-\lambda}}{n!} + \sum_{n=0}^{\infty} \frac{\lambda^n e^{-\lambda}}{n!} \right)$$

$$= \lambda[E(X)+1] = \lambda^2 + \lambda.$$

Hence $V(X) = \lambda^2 + \lambda - 2\lambda^2 + \lambda^2 = \lambda.$

5-23. If the first 11 occurs on the eighth roll, there are 7 failures first, and $p = \frac{1}{18}$ and $q = \frac{17}{18}$.

$$P(X=7) = \left(\frac{17}{18}\right)^7 \left(\frac{1}{18}\right) = .0372$$

5-24. (a) The number of initial failures is 4, and $p = \frac{1}{4}, q = \frac{3}{4}$.

$$P(X=4) = \left(\frac{3}{4}\right)^4 \left(\frac{1}{4}\right) = .0791$$

(b) The number of initial failures is 9, and $p = \frac{1}{13}, q = \frac{12}{13}$.

$$P(X=9) = \left(\frac{12}{13}\right)^9 \left(\frac{1}{13}\right) = .0374$$

5-25.   Probability of an ace is $p = \frac{1}{13}$, so $q = \frac{12}{13}$.

$$E(X) = \frac{q}{p} = \frac{12/13}{1/13} = 12$$

$$V(X) = \frac{q}{p^2} = \frac{12/13}{(1/13)^2} = 156$$

5-26.   (a) If the fifth patient is the first one with the disease, then there are 4 initial failures.

$$P(X=4) = (.85)^4(.15) = .0783$$

(b)   For the second part there are 9 initial failures.

$$P(X=9) = (.85)^9(.15) = .0347$$

5-27.   (a) If the third heart appears on the tenth draw, there are 7 failures.

$$P(X=7) = C(7+3-1, 3-1)q^7 p^3 = C(9,2)\left(\tfrac{3}{4}\right)^7 \left(\tfrac{1}{4}\right)^3 = .0751$$

(b) If X is the number of non-hearts drawn before the fifth heart, then

$$E(X) = \frac{rq}{p} = 5\frac{(3/4)}{(1/4)} = 15.$$

5-28.   (a) If the fourth 6 appears on the twentieth roll, there are 16 initial failures.

$$P(X=16) = C(19,3)\left(\tfrac{5}{6}\right)^{16} \left(\tfrac{1}{6}\right)^4 = .0404$$

(b) If X is the number of failures before the fourth 6, then

$$E(X) = \frac{rq}{p} = 4\frac{(5/6)}{(1/6)} = 20.$$

The expected total number of rolls is $20 + 4 = 24$.

5-29.   Let X be the number of failures before the fifth 6.

$$E(X) = \frac{rq}{p} = 5\frac{(5/6)}{(1/6)} = 25$$

$$V(X) = \frac{rq}{p^2} = 5\frac{(5/6)}{(1/6)^2} = 150$$

5-30.   If the fifth success occurs on the sixteenth call, there are 11 initial failures.

$$P(X=11) = C(15,4)(.8)^{11}(.2)^5 = .0375$$

5-31.   Number of successes needed is $\frac{2000}{250} = 8$. If X is the number of failures before the eighth success, then

$$E(X) = 8\frac{(.8)}{(.2)} = 32,$$

The total expected number of calls is $32 + 8 = 40$.

5-32.   (a) There would be 12 failures before the third success.

$$P(X=12) = C(14,2)(.85)^{12}(.15)^3 = .0437$$

(b) If X is the number patients without the disease tested before the sixth with, then

$$E(X) = 6\frac{(.85)}{(.15)} = 34.$$

5-33. The outcome X is a discrete uniform random variable with
$p(x) = \frac{1}{6}$, $x = 1,2,3,4,5,6$.

$$E(X) = \frac{1+2+3+4+5+6}{6} = \frac{21}{6} = 3.5$$

$$V(X) = \frac{(1-3.5)^2 + (2-3.5)^2 + (3-3.5)^2 + (4-3.5)^2 + (5-3.5)^2 + (6-3.5)^2}{6}$$
$$= \frac{6.25+2.25+.25+.25+2.25+6.25}{6}$$
$$= \frac{17.5}{6} = \frac{35}{12}$$

5-34. Let Y be the number on the ball chosen. Y is a discrete uniform
random variable, with $n = 25$ and $p(n) = \frac{1}{25}$, $n = 1,2,...,25$, and
$X = 1000Y$.

$$E(X) = 1000E(Y) = \frac{1000(26)}{2} = \$13,000$$

$$V(X) = 1000^2 V(Y) = \frac{1000^2(25^2-1)}{12} = 1000^2(52) = \sigma^2$$

$$\sigma = \$7,211.10$$

5-35. Let X be the discrete uniform random variable with $p(x) = \frac{1}{n}$
for $x = 1,2,3,...,n$.

$$E(X) = \sum xp(x) = \frac{1+2+\cdots+n}{n} = \frac{1}{n} \cdot \frac{n(n+1)}{2} = \frac{n+1}{2} = \mu.$$

$$V(X) = E\left[(X-\mu)^2\right] = E(X^2 - 2\mu X + \mu^2)$$
$$= \sum(k^2 - 2\mu k + \mu^2)p(k)$$
$$= \sum k^2 p(k) - 2\mu \sum kp(k) + \mu^2 \sum p(k)$$

The second term is $-2\mu E(X) = -2\mu^2$, and the last term is μ^2.

The sum of these two is $-\mu^2 = \dfrac{(n+1)^2}{4}$.

$$\sum k^2 p(k) = \dfrac{1^2 + 2^2 + \cdots + n^2}{n}$$

$$= \dfrac{1}{n} \cdot \dfrac{n(n+1)(2n+1)}{6} = \dfrac{2n^2 + 3n + 1}{6}$$

$$V(X) = \dfrac{2n^2 + 3n + 1}{6} - \dfrac{n^2 + 2n + 1}{4}$$

$$= \dfrac{8n^2 + 12n + 4 - 6n^2 - 12n - 6}{24} = \dfrac{n^2 - 1}{12}$$

5-36.   This is a binomial distribution problem. There are $n = 20$ independent trials in 20 years, with $p = \Pr(\text{hurricane}) = .05$ in each year. The binomial random variable X is the number of hurricanes in 20 years. We are asked to find

$$P(X < 3) = P(X=0) + P(X=1) + P(X=2)$$

$$= .95^{20} + \binom{20}{1}.95^{19}(.05) + \binom{20}{2}.95^{18}(.05)^2$$

$$= .92452$$

5-37.   Denote the random variables for the number of participants completing in each group by A and B. The probability we need is

$$P\big[(A \geq 9 \,\&\, B < 9) \text{ or } (B \geq 9 \,\&\, A < 9)\big]$$

$$= P(A \geq 9 \,\&\, B < 9) + P(B \geq 9 \,\&\, A < 9)$$

$$\underset{Ind}{=} P(A \geq 9)P(B < 9) + P(B \geq 9)P(A < 9)$$

Since the two groups are independent and have identical binomial probability distributions, we can analyze the random variable A and obtain all the information we need. The random variable A is binomial with $n = 10$ independent trials and probability of completion $p = .8$. Direct calculation shows that

$$P(A \geq 9) = P(A = 10) + P(A = 9)$$

$$= .8^{10} + \binom{10}{9}.8^9(.2) = .376$$

It follows that

$$P(A < 9) = 1 - P(A \geq 9) = .624$$

$$P(B \geq 9) = .376$$

$$P(B < 9) = .624$$

$$P(A \geq 9)P(B < 9) + P(B \geq 9)P(A < 9)$$

$$= .376(.624) + .376(.624)$$

$$= .469$$

5-38.   This is a Bayes theorem problem, with a binomial probability component. Let X denote the event that the shipment came from company X, and I denote the event that exactly one vial out of 30 tested is ineffective. We are asked to find $P(X | I)$.

Note that if the shipment is from company X, the number of defectives in 30 components is a binomial random variable with $n = 30$ and $p = .1$. The probability of one defective in a batch of 30 from X is

$$P(I | X) = \binom{30}{1}(.1)(.9^{29}) = .141$$

Similarly if the shipment is not from company X, the number of defectives in 30 components is a binomial random variable with $n = 30$ and $p = .02$. The probability of one defective in a batch of 30 that is not from X is

$$P(I |\sim X) = \binom{30}{1}(.02)(.98^{29}) = .334$$

We will display the situation the following tree diagram.

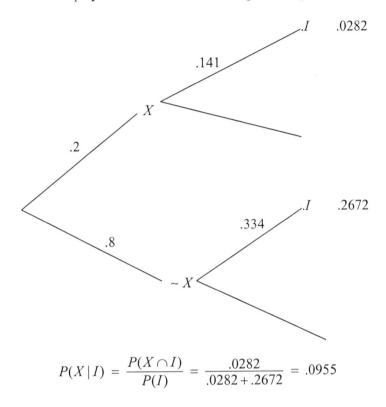

$$P(X \mid I) = \frac{P(X \cap I)}{P(I)} = \frac{.0282}{.0282 + .2672} = .0955$$

5-39.   We need to find the variance of the Poisson distribution –i.e., the parameter λ. Let X denote the Poisson random variable for the number of claims. The statement that "policyholders are three times as likely to file two claims as to file four claims" tells us that

$$P(X = 2) = 3P(X = 4).$$

Thus

$$\frac{e^{-\lambda}\lambda^2}{2!} = 3\left(\frac{e^{-\lambda}\lambda^4}{4!}\right)$$

$$4\lambda^2 = \lambda^4$$

The Poisson parameter must be positive, so our solution is the positive root of the last equation.

$$\lambda = 2$$

5-40.   *Note. This is a tougher problem.* Let L denote the amount paid and N the number of storms. We need to find $E(L)$. To do this we first go directly to the definition of expected value.

$$E(L) = 0 \cdot P(N=0) + \sum_{n=1}^{\infty} 10,000(n-1)P(N=n)$$

$$= \sum_{n=1}^{\infty} 10,000(n-1)P(N=n)$$

This differs by only one term from

$$E\big[10,000(N-1)\big] = -10,000 \cdot P(N=0)$$

$$+ \sum_{n=1}^{\infty} 10,000(n-1)P(N=n)$$

$$= -10,000 \cdot P(N=0) + E(L).$$

It is easy to evaluate $E\big[10,000(N-1)\big]$ from the given information.

$$E\big[10,000(N-1)\big] = 10,000\big[E(N)-1\big]$$

$$= 10,000(1.5-1) = 5,000$$

It follows that

$$-10,000 \cdot P(N=0) + E(L) = 5,000$$

$$E(L) = 5,000 + 10,000 P(N=0)$$

$$= 5,000 + 10,000 e^{-1.5} = 7,231$$

5-41. In order to work with this recursive definition of the probability distribution, we need to find the starting point p_0. We will look at the first few terms of the distribution to get an idea of what is going on. The table below shows the values of the probability distribution for $n = 0, 1, 2, 3$.

n	0	1	2	3
p_n	p_0	$p_0\left(\frac{1}{5}\right)$	$p_0\left(\frac{1}{5}\right)^2$	$p_0\left(\frac{1}{5}\right)^3$

We will find p_0 using the fact that the sum of the probabilities is 1. The pattern above shows that

$$1 = p_0\left(1 + \frac{1}{5} + \left(\frac{1}{5}\right)^2 + \left(\frac{1}{5}\right)^3 + \cdots + \left(\frac{1}{5}\right)^n + \cdots\right)$$

$$= p_0\left(\frac{1}{1-\frac{1}{5}}\right) = \frac{5}{4}p_0$$

Thus $p_0 = \frac{4}{5}$. We are asked to find

$$P(N > 1) = 1 - P(N \leq 1) = 1 - \left[\frac{4}{5} + \frac{4}{5}\left(\frac{1}{5}\right)\right] = .04$$

Note. Some students bypassed the geometric series calculation to find p_0 by observing that the probability distribution had the form of a geometric distribution with $q = \frac{1}{5}$, so that it must be true that $p_0 = p = \frac{4}{5}$.

CHAPTER 6

6-1.

x	0	1	2	3
$p(x)$	.69	.23	.07	.01

(a) $E(X) = 0(.69) + 1(.23) + 2(.07) + 3(.01) = .40$

$E(500X + 50) = 500E(X) + 50 = 250$

(b) $E(X^2) = 0(.69) + 1(.23) + 4(.07) + 9(.01) = .60$

(c) $E(X^3) = 0(.69) + 1(.23) + 8(.07) + 27(.01) = 1.06$

6-2. The following table relates to the rolling of a pair of dice.

X	$p(x)$	$xp(x)$	$x^2 p(x)$
2	1/36	2/36	4/36
3	2/36	6/36	18/36
4	3/36	12/36	48/36
5	4/36	20/36	100/36
6	5/36	30/36	180/36
7	6/36	42/36	294/36
8	5/36	40/36	320/36
9	4/36	36/36	324/36
10	3/36	30/36	300/36
11	2/36	22/36	242/36
12	1/36	12/36	144/36

$E(X) = \Sigma xp(x) = \frac{252}{36} = 7$

$E(X^2) = \Sigma x^2 p(x) = \frac{1974}{36} = 54.8333$

$V(X) = E(X^2) - E(X)^2 = 54.8333 - 49 = 5.8333$

6-3.   Using the utility function $u(x) = \ln(x+1)$ we have the following:

Method 1

Wealth w	0	10,000
$u(w) = \ln(w+1)$	0	$\ln(10,001)$
$p(w)$	.10	.90

Method 2

Wealth w	0	9,025
$u(w) = \ln(w+1)$	0	$\ln(9,026)$
$p(w)$	.02	.98

$$E\left[u(W_1)\right] = .10(0) + .90\ln(10,001) = 8.289$$

$$E\left[u(W_2)\right] = .02(0) + .98\ln(9,026) = 8.926$$

Method 2 gives a higher expected utility.

6-4.   This is primarily an exercise for the reader to observe the precision of his or her particular computer or calculator.

$$E(X) = 1,000,000,000 = \mu$$
$$V(X) = E\left[(X-\mu)^2\right] = \left(\tfrac{1}{3}\right)(.01+0+.01) = .00\overline{66}$$

The value you get using $V(X) = E(X^2) - E(X)^2$ will vary from calculator to calculator.

6-5. Let X be the binomial random variable with n trials and $P(S) = p$.

$$M_x(t) = E(e^{tX}) = \Sigma e^{tx} p(x)$$
$$= \Sigma e^{tx} C(n,x) p^x q^{n-x} = \Sigma C(n,x)(e^t p)^x q^{n-x}$$
$$(q+p)^n = \Sigma C(n,x) p^x q^{n-x}$$

If we replace p with pe^t, we get $M_x(t) = (q+pe^t)^n$.

6-6. For the Poisson random variable with rate λ,

$$M_X(t) = e^{\lambda(e^t-1)}.$$
$$M'_X(t) = \lambda e^t e^{\lambda(e^t-1)}, \quad M'_X(0) = \lambda(1)(1) = \lambda = E(X)$$
$$M''_X(t) = e^{\lambda(e^t-1)}\left(\lambda e^t + (\lambda e^t)^2\right) \quad M''_X(0) = \lambda + \lambda^2 = E(X^2)$$
$$V(X) = E(X^2) - E(X)^2 = \lambda$$

6-7. For the geometric random variable with $P(S) = p$,

$$M_X(t) = \frac{p}{1-qe^t}, \quad \text{and} \quad M'_X(t) = \frac{-p(-qe^t)}{(1-qe^t)^2}.$$

$$E(X) = M'_X(0) = \frac{pq}{(1-q)^2} = \frac{pq}{p^2} = \frac{q}{p}$$

$$M''_X(t) = \frac{pqe^t(1-qe^t) + 2pq^2 e^{2t}}{(1-qe^t)^3}$$

$$E(X^2) = M''_X(0) = \frac{pq(1-q) + 2pq^2}{(1-q)^3}$$
$$= \frac{p^2 q + 2pq^2}{p^3} = \frac{pq+2q^2}{p^2} -$$

$$V(X) = E(X^2) - E(X)^2 = \frac{pq+2q^2}{p^2} - \frac{q^2}{p^2}$$
$$= \frac{pq+q^2}{p^2} = \frac{q(p+q)}{p^2} = \frac{q}{p^2}$$

6-8.   For the negative binomial random variable with $P(S) = p$ and X the number of failures before r successes,

$$M_X(t) = \frac{p^r}{(1-qe^t)^r}$$

$$M'_X(t) = \frac{rp^r qe^t}{(1-qe^t)^{r+1}}$$

$$E(X) = M'_X(0) = \frac{rp^r q}{(1-q)^{r+1}}$$

$$= \frac{rp^r q}{p^{r+1}}$$

$$= \frac{rq}{p}$$

$$M''_X(t) = \frac{rp^r qe^t(1-qe^t) + r(r+1)p^r q^2 e^{2t}}{(1-qe^t)^{r+2}}$$

$$E(X^2) = M''_X(0) = \frac{rp^r q(1-q) + r(r+1)p^r q^2}{(1-q)^{r+2}}$$

$$= \frac{rpq + r(r+1)q^2}{p^2}$$

$$V(X) = E(X^2) - E(X)^2 = \frac{rpq + r(r+1)q^2}{p^2} - \frac{r^2 q^2}{p^2}$$

$$= \frac{rpq + rq^2}{p^2}$$

$$= \frac{rq(p+q)}{p^2}$$

$$= \frac{rq}{p^2}$$

6-9. For the discrete uniform random variable, $p(x) = \frac{1}{n}$, for $x = 1, 2, ..., n$.

(a) $M_X(t) = \sum_{x=1}^{n} e^{xt} p(t) = \frac{1}{n} \sum_{x=1}^{n} e^{xt} = \frac{e^t(1-e^{nt})}{n(1-e^t)}$, $t \neq 0$

(b) $M_X'(t) = \frac{1}{n} \sum_{x=1}^{n} x e^{xt}$

$E(X) = M_X'(0) = \frac{1}{n} \sum_{x=1}^{n} x = \frac{1}{n} \cdot \frac{n(n+1)}{2} = \frac{n+1}{2}$

$M_X''(t) = \sum_{x=1}^{n} x^2 e^{xt}$

$E(X^2) = M_X''(0) = \frac{1}{n} \sum_{x=1}^{n} x^2 = \frac{1}{n} \cdot \frac{n(n+1)(2n+1)}{6}$

$\qquad\qquad\qquad\qquad\qquad\quad = \frac{(n+1)(2n+1)}{6}$

$V(X) = E(X^2) - E(X)^2 \quad = \frac{(n+1)(2n+1)}{6} - \frac{(n+1)^2}{4}$

$\qquad\qquad\qquad\qquad\qquad\quad = \frac{n^2-1}{12}$

6-10. $M_X(t) = \sum e^{xt} p(x) = .42 + .30e^t + .17e^{2t} + .11e^{3t}$

$M_X'(t) = .30e^t + .17(2)e^{2t} + .11(3)e^{3t}$

$E(X) = M_X'(0) = .30 + .34 + .33 = .97$

$M_X''(t) = .30e^t + .17(4)e^{2t} + .11(9)e^{3t}$

$E(X^2) = M_X''(0) = .30 + .68 + .99 = 1.97$

6-11. $M_X(at) = E(e^{atX}) = \sum e^{atx} p(x)$

$M_{aX+b}(t) = E\left(e^{(aX+b)t}\right) = \sum e^{axt+bt} p(x) = e^{bt} \sum e^{axt} p(x)$

$\qquad\qquad\qquad\qquad\qquad\qquad\qquad = e^{bt} M_X(at)$

6-12. For the binomial random variable with n trials and $P(s) = p$,

$M_X(t) = (q + pe^t)^n$.

If $n = 8$ and $p = .6$, then $M_X(t) = (.4 + .6e^t)^8$

If $Y = 3X + 4$, then $M_Y(t) = e^{4t}(.4 + .6e^{3t})^8$

6-13.   The moment generating function for the negative binomial

distribution is $M_X(t) = \left(\dfrac{p}{1-qe^t}\right)^r$.

Therefore $\left(\dfrac{.70}{1-.3e^t}\right)^5$ is the moment generating of the negative

binomial distribution with $r = 5$ and $p = .70$.

6-14.   Successive applications of the linear congruence $y = 9x+11$
(mod 16) yields the following table.

k	x_k	$9x_k + 11$	$9x_k + 11\,(\text{mod}16)$
1	6	65	1
2	1	20	4
3	4	47	15
4	15	146	2
5	2	29	13
6	13	128	0
7	0	11	11
8	11	110	14
9	14	137	9
10	9	92	12
11	12	119	7
12	7	74	10
13	10	101	5
14	5	56	8
15	8	83	3
16	3	38	6

The following table is for the simulations in Exercises 6-15 and 6-16. In Exercise 6-15, if the random number $x < .40$, the result was a success. Otherwise it was a failure. In Exercise 6-16, if the random number $x < .50$, the result was a head. Otherwise it was a tail.

Trial	Random Number	S or F	H or T
1	.5619	F	T
2	.4500	F	H
3	.3566	S	H
4	.5844	F	T
5	.8638	F	T
6	.9983	F	T
7	.0225	S	H
8	.8026	F	T
9	.3516	S	H
10	.4584	F	H
11	.7855	F	T
12	.9955	F	T
13	.6558	F	T
14	.1280	S	H
15	.3908	S	H
16	.3729	S	H
17	.1326	S	H
18	.9246	F	T
19	.6867	F	T
20	.9638	F	T

6-15.   In these 20 trials there are 7 successes.

6-16.   The first trial (first set of 5 numbers) yields 2 heads, the second trial yields 3 heads, the third trial yields 2 heads, and the fourth trial yields 2 heads.

6-17. Let X be the amount paid by the insurance company and K the number of days of rain. The next table shows the amount paid by the number of days of rain.

Days of rain k	0	1	≥ 2
Amount paid	0	1000	2000

We need a probability for each value of k in the table. The distribution of K is Poisson with $\lambda = .6$. Thus

$$P(K=0) = e^{-.6} = .54881 \qquad P(K=1) = e^{-.6}(.6) = .32929$$

$$P(K \geq 2) = 1 - \left[P(K=0) + P(K=1) \right]$$
$$= 1 - \left[.54881 + .32929 \right] = .12190$$

We need to find the standard deviation of X. We will first find $V(X) = E(X^2) - E(X)^2$.

$$E(X) = .32929(1000) + .12190(2000) = 573.09$$

$$E(X^2) = .32929(1000)^2 + .12190(2000)^2 = 816,890$$

$$V(X) = E(X^2) - E(X)^2$$
$$= 816,890 - (573.09)^2 = 488,457.85$$

The standard deviation of X is

$$\sigma_X = \sqrt{488,457.85} = 698.9$$

6-18. Since each X_i can be only 0 or 1, the product $Y = X_1 X_2 X_3$ can be only 0 or 1. In addition, Y is 1 if and only if all of the X_i are 1. Thus

$$P(Y=1) = \left(\frac{2}{3} \right)^3 = \frac{8}{27}$$

$$P(Y=0) = 1 - P(Y=1) = 1 - \left(\frac{2}{3} \right)^3 = \frac{19}{27}$$

$$M_Y(t) = E(e^{Yt}) = \frac{19}{27} e^{0t} + \frac{8}{27} e^{1t} = \frac{19}{27} + \frac{8}{27} e^t .$$

CHAPTER 7

7-1. The function $f(x) = 1.5x + .25$, for $0 \le x \le 1$, and 0 elsewhere.

(a) Clearly $f(x) \ge 0$ for all x, so we only need to show that the area under the curve is 1.

$$\int_{-\infty}^{\infty} f(x)dx = \int_{0}^{1}(1.5x+.25)dx = (.75x^2+.25x)\Big|_{0}^{1}$$
$$= .75 + .25 = 1$$

Hence $f(x)$ is a probability density function.

(b) $F(x) = P(X \le x) = \int_{0}^{x}(1.5t+.25)dt = (.75x^2+.25x)$ for $0 \le x \le 1$. $F(x)=0$ for $x<0$, and $F(x)=1$ for $x>1$.

(c) $P(0 \le X \le 1/2) = F(.5) - F(0)$
$$= \left[.75(.5)^2 + .25(.5)\right] - [0+0] = .3125$$
$P(1/4 \le X \le 3/4) = F(.75) - F(.25)$
$$= \left[.75(.75)^2 + .25(.75)\right]$$
$$- \left[.75(.25)^2 + .25(.25)\right]$$
$$= .609375 - .109375 = .50$$

7-2. (a) We need to find a so that the area under the curve is 1.

$$\int_{-\infty}^{\infty} f(x)dx = \int_{0}^{\infty} a(e^{-2x}-e^{-3x})dx = a\left[-\left(\tfrac{1}{2}\right)e^{-2x}+\left(\tfrac{1}{3}\right)e^{-3x}\right]\Big|_{0}^{\infty}$$
$$= a(0) - a\left(-\tfrac{1}{2}+\tfrac{1}{3}\right) = \tfrac{a}{6}$$

For this to be a probability density function $\tfrac{a}{6}=1$, and $a=6$.

(b) $P(X \le 1) = 6\int_{0}^{1}(e^{-2x}-e^{-3x})dx = (-3e^{-2x}+2e^{-3x})\Big|_{0}^{1}$
$$= (-3e^{-2}+2e^{-3})-(-3+2) = -.3064+1 = .6936$$

7-3. $P(.10 \leq X \leq .60) = \int_{.1}^{.6} f(x)dx$

$= \int_{.1}^{.2} 25xdx + \int_{.2}^{.6} 1.5625(1-x)dx$

$= 12.5x^2\Big|_{.1}^{.2} - .78125(1-x)^2\Big|_{.2}^{.6} = .375 + .375 = .75$

7-4.   (a) $\int_{-\infty}^{\infty} f(x)dx = \int_{0}^{\infty} \frac{a}{1+x^2} = a\tan^{-1}(x)\Big|_{0}^{\infty} = a\left(\frac{\pi}{2}\right)$

For this to be a probability density function, $a\left(\frac{\pi}{2}\right)$ must

equal 1, so $a = \frac{2}{\pi}$.

(b) $P(X \leq 1) = \left(\frac{2}{\pi}\right)\int_{0}^{1} \frac{1}{1+x^2}dx$ $\left(\frac{2}{\pi}\right)[\tan^{-1}(1) - \tan^{-1}(0)]$

$= \left(\frac{2}{\pi}\right)\left(\frac{\pi}{4} - 0\right) = \frac{1}{2}$

7-5.   For the density function in Exercise 7-1, $F(x) = .75x^2 + .25x$.

To find x_p we need to solve $F(x) = p$.

For $p = .25$ we have $.75x^2 + .25x = .25$, or $3x^2 + x = 1$.

The positive solution of this equation is $x = .4343 = x_{.25}$.

For $p = .50$ we have $.75x^2 + .25x = .5$, or $3x^2 + x = 2$.

The positive solution of this equation is $x = \frac{2}{3} = x_{.50}$..

For $p = .75$ we have $.75x^2 + .25x = .75$, or $3x^2 + x = 3$.

The positive solution of the equation is $x = .8471 = x_{.75}$.

7-6.   If $f(x) = e^x$ for $0 \le x \le \ln 2$, then

$$F(x) = \int_0^x e^t \, dt = e^x - 1.$$

(a) Solving $F(x) = p$ when $p = .50$ we get

$$e^x - 1 = .50, \text{ or } e^x = 1.5.$$

The solution of this equation is $x = \ln 1.5 = .4055 = x_{.50}$.

Solving $F(x) = p$ when $p = .90$ we get

$$e^x - 1 = .90, \text{ or } e^x = 1.9.$$

The solution of this equation is $x = \ln 1.9 = .6419 = x_{.90}$.

(b) The mode of this distribution is the value of x for which the density function, $f(x)$, is a maximum. Since e^x is increasing, the maximum occurs at the right hand endpoint, $x = \ln 2$.

7-7.   For the density function in Exercise 7-3, if $0 \le x \le .2$, then

$$F(x) = \int_0^x 25t \, dt = 12.5x^2, \text{ and } F(.20) = .50.$$

Hence the median is .20.

For $.20 < x \le 1$,
$$\begin{aligned}
F(X) &= .50 + 1.5625 \int_{.2}^x (1-t)dt \\
&= .50 + 1.5625 \left(t - \tfrac{t^2}{2} \right) \Big|_{.2}^x \\
&= .50 + 1.5625 \left(x - \tfrac{x^2}{2} - .18 \right) \\
&= .50 + 1.5625x - .78125x^2 - .28125.
\end{aligned}$$

Solving $F(x) = .80$ we get

$$.78125x^2 - 1.5625x + .58125 = 0.$$

The solution to this equation in $(.2, 1)$ is $x = .4940 = x_{.80}$.

7-8.   For the density function in Exercise 7-1:

$$E(X) = \int_0^1 x(1.5x + .25) \, dx = \int_0^1 (1.5x^2 + .25x) \, dx$$

$$= (.5x^3 + .125x^2)\Big|_0^1 = .625$$

$$E(X^2) = \int_0^1 x^2 (1.5x + .25) \, dx = \int_0^1 (1.5x^3 + .25x^2) \, dx$$

$$= \left[\left(\tfrac{1.5}{4}\right) x^4 + \left(\tfrac{.25}{3}\right) x^3 \right]\Big|_0^1 = .45833$$

$$V(X) = E(X^2) - E(X)^2 = .45833 - .625^2 = .0677$$

7-9. $$E(X) = \int_0^{.2} x(25x)dx + \int_{.2}^1 1.5625x(1-x) \, dx$$

$$= \int_0^{.2} 25x^2 dx + 1.5625 \int_{.2}^1 (x - x^2) \, dx$$

$$= \left(\tfrac{25}{3}\right) x^3 \Big|_0^{.2} + 1.5625 \left(\tfrac{x^2}{2} - \tfrac{x^3}{3}\right)\Big|_{.2}^1 = .066\overline{6} + .233\overline{3} = .30$$

7-10.   For the density function $f(x) = .75(1-x^2)$ if $-1 \le x \le 1$ and 0 elsewhere,

$$E(X) = .75 \int_{-1}^1 x(1-x^2) \, dx = .75\left(\tfrac{x^2}{2} - \tfrac{x^4}{4}\right)\Big|_{-1}^1 = 0.$$

$$F(x) = \int_{-1}^x .75(1-t^2) \, dt = .75\left(t - \tfrac{t^3}{3}\right)\Big|_{-1}^x = .75x - .25x^3 + .50$$

To find the median we have to solve $f(x) = .50$.

$$.75x - .25x^3 + .50 = .50$$
$$.25(3x - x^3) = 0$$

The only solution in $[-1,1]$ is 0, so the median is 0, and the mean and the median are the same.

7-11.   For the density function $f(x) = \dfrac{2}{\pi(1+x^2)}$ for $x \geq 0$,

$$E(X) = \frac{2}{\pi}\int_0^\infty \frac{x}{1+x^2}\,dx = \left(\frac{1}{\pi}\right)\ln(1+x^2)\Big|_0^\infty.$$

This does not have a finite value, so $E(X)$ does not exist.

7-12.   Since $f(x)$ is proportional to $(10+x)^{-2}$, $f(x) = k(10+x)^{-2}$. We
        can find k using the fact that the total area bounded by the x-axis
        and the graph of $f(x)$ between $x = 0$ and $x = 40$ is 1.

$$1 = \int_0^{40} k(10+x)^{-2}\,dx = -k(10+x)^{-1}\Big|_0^{40} = -k\left(\frac{1}{50}-\frac{1}{10}\right) = k\frac{4}{50}$$

$$k = \frac{50}{4} = 12.5 \;\rightarrow\; f(x) = 12.5(10+x)^{-2}.$$

We need to find

$$P(X<6) = \int_0^6 12.5(10+x)^{-2}\,dx = -12.5(10+x)^{-1}\Big|_0^6$$

$$= -12.5\left(\frac{1}{16}-\frac{1}{10}\right) = .46875$$

7-13.   Recall that the $100p^{th}$ percentile of X is the number x_p defined by
        $F(x_p) = p$. We are asked to find the difference $x_{.70} - x_{.30}$. To
        begin, we must find an expression for $F(x)$. For $x \geq 200$,

$$F(x) = \int_{200}^x \frac{2.5(200)^{2.5}}{u^{3.5}}\,du$$

$$= 2.5(200)^{2.5}\frac{u^{-2.5}}{-2.5}\Big|_{200}^x$$

$$= 2.5(200)^{2.5}\frac{x^{-2.5}}{-2.5} - 2.5(200)^{2.5}\frac{200^{-2.5}}{-2.5} = 1 - \left(\frac{200}{x}\right)^{2.5}$$

Since we have to find two percentiles, we will derive a general
formula for the $100p^{th}$ percentile of X. The defining equation is

$$F(x_p) = p = 1-\left(\frac{200}{x_p}\right)^{2.5} \;\to\; (1-p) = \left(\frac{200}{x_p}\right)^{2.5} \;\to\;$$

$$(1-p)^{(1/2.5)} = \left(\frac{200}{x_p}\right) \;\to\; x_p = \frac{200}{(1-p)^{1/2.5}} = \frac{200}{(1-p)^{0.4}}$$

Thus

$$x_{.70} - x_{.30} = \frac{200}{.30^{0.4}} - \frac{200}{.70^{0.4}} = 93.06$$

7-14. Since $f(x)$ is proportional to $(1+x)^{-4}$, $f(x) = k(1+x)^{-4}$. We can find k using the fact that the total area bounded by the x-axis and the graph of $f(x)$ is 1.

$$1 = \int_0^\infty k(1+x)^{-4}\,dx = k\left.\frac{(1+x)^{-3}}{-3}\right|_0^\infty$$

$$k = 3 \;\to\; f(x) = 3(1+x)^{-4}.$$

Thus

$$E(X) = \int_0^\infty 3x(1+x)^{-4}\,dx.$$

This is more a test of your integration skills than a probability problem. You need to make the substitution $u = (1+x)$, which gives $x = u-1$ and $du = dx$. It is very important to note that as x goes from 0 to ∞, then $u = (1+x)$ goes from 1 to ∞. This changes the limits of integration.

$$E(X) = \int_0^\infty 3x(1+x)^{-4}\,dx = \int_1^\infty 3(u-1)u^{-4}\,du$$

$$= 3\int_1^\infty \left(u^{-3} - u^{-4}\right)du$$

$$= 3\left.\left(\frac{u^{-2}}{-2} - \frac{u^{-3}}{-3}\right)\right|_1^\infty$$

$$= 3\left[0 - \left(\frac{1}{-2} - \frac{1}{-3}\right)\right] = \frac{1}{2}$$

7-15. We must find

$$E(X) = \int_{-\infty}^{\infty} f(x)dx = \int_{-2}^{4} x\frac{|x|}{10}\,dx.$$

This must be done piecewise, since

$$|x| = \begin{cases} -x & \text{for } x < 0 \\ x & \text{for } x \geq 0 \end{cases}.$$

Thus the integral becomes

$$E(X) = \int_{-2}^{4} x\frac{|x|}{10}\,dx = \int_{-2}^{0}\frac{-x^2}{10}\,dx + \int_{0}^{4}\frac{x^2}{10}\,dx$$

$$= \left.\frac{-x^3}{30}\right|_{-2}^{0} + \left.\frac{x^3}{30}\right|_{0}^{4}$$

$$= \frac{-8}{30} + \frac{64}{30} = \frac{56}{30} = \frac{28}{15}$$

7-16. We need to find

$$P(X > 16 \mid X > 8) = \frac{P(X > 16 \ \& \ X > 8)}{P(X > 8)} = \frac{P(X > 16)}{P(X > 8)}.$$

Since we need to find two expressions of the form $P(X > k)$, we will calculate this in general for $0 < k < 20$.

$$P(X > k) = \int_{k}^{20} .005(20-x)dx = \left.-.005\frac{(20-x)^2}{2}\right|_{k}^{20}$$

$$= .0025(20-k)^2$$

It follows that

$$P(X>16 \mid X>8) = \frac{P(X>16)}{P(X>8)} = \frac{.0025(20-16)^2}{.0025(20-8)^2} = \frac{16}{144} = \frac{1}{9}$$

7-17. We need to find

$$P(X < 2 \mid X \geq 1.5) \;=\; \frac{P(X < 2 \ \& \ X \geq 1.5)}{P(X \geq 1.5)} \;=\; \frac{F(2) - F(1.5)}{1 - F(1.5)}.$$

Since we need to find two expressions involving $F(X)$, we will calculate this in general.

$$F(x) \;=\; P(X \leq x) \;=\; \int_{1}^{x} 3u^{-4}\,du \;=\; -u^{-3}\Big|_{1}^{x} \;=\; 1 - x^{-3}$$

It follows that

$$P(X < 2 \mid X \geq 1.5) \;=\; \frac{F(2) - F(1.5)}{1 - F(1.5)} \;=\; \frac{1.5^{-3} - 2^{-3}}{1.5^{-3}} \;=\; .57813.$$

CHAPTER 8

8-1. For the uniform distribution on $[a,b]$, $f(x) = \frac{1}{b-a}$.

$$E(X^2) = \int_a^b \frac{x^2}{b-a}\,dx = \frac{b^3-a^3}{3(b-a)} = \left(\frac{1}{3}\right)(b^2+ab+a^2)$$

$$\begin{aligned}
V(X) &= E(X^2) - E(X)^2 \\
&= \left(\frac{1}{3}\right)(b^2+ab+a^2) - \left(\frac{1}{4}\right)(b^2+2ab+a^2) \\
&= \frac{(b^2-2ab+a^2)}{12}2 = \frac{(b-a)^2}{12}
\end{aligned}$$

8-2. If T is uniformly distributed on $[0,100]$:

$$E(T) = \frac{100+0}{2} = 50$$

$$V(T) = \frac{(100-0)^2}{12} = 833.33$$

8-3. Let T be the time (in minutes from 5:00) that the baby is born; then T is uniformly distributed on $[0,60]$.

$$F(t) = P(T \le t) = \frac{t}{60}$$

$$P(15 \le T \le 25) = F(25) - F(15) = \frac{25}{60} - \frac{15}{60} = \frac{1}{6}$$

8-4. Since X is uniform on $[-.50, .50]$,

$$F(x) = \frac{x-(-.50)}{.50-(-.50)} = x + .50.$$

(a) $P(-.10 \le X \le .20) = F(.20) - F(-.10) = .70 - .40 = .30$

(b) $V(X) = \frac{[.50-(-.50)]^2}{12} = \frac{1}{12}$

8-5. (a) T is uniform on $(35,50)$, so

$$E(T) = \frac{50+35}{2} = 42.5$$
$$V(T) = \frac{(50-35)^2}{12} = \frac{15^2}{12} = 18.75$$

(b) The time at which 60 percent will be finished, $t_{.60}$, is the solution of $F(t) = .60$.

$$F(t) = \frac{t-35}{15}, \text{ so we solve}$$
$$\frac{t-35}{15} = .60$$
$$t = 44.$$

8-6. For y in $[c,d]$ and T uniform on $[a,b]$:

$$P(Y \le y) = P(T \le y \mid c \le T \le d)$$
$$= \frac{P(c \le T \le y)}{P(c \le T \le d)}$$
$$= \frac{(y-c)/(b-a)}{(d-c)/(b-a)} = \frac{y-c}{d-c}$$

Hence Y has a uniform distribution over $[c,d]$.

8-7. (a) Since T is uniform on $[40,100]$ we have

$$E(T) = \frac{100+40}{2} = 70$$
$$V(T) = \frac{(100-40)^2}{12} = 300$$

(b) $P(T > 57) = 1 - P(T \le 57) = 1 - \frac{17}{60} = .7167$

8-8.   Let X and Y be the random variables of the ages at time of death for the 45-year-old and the 50-year-old, respectively. Then X is uniform on $[45,100]$ and Y is uniform on $[50,100]$.

The probability that the 45-year-old dies in the next 20 years is

$$P(X \le 65) = \frac{65-45}{100-45} = \frac{20}{55} = \frac{4}{11}.$$

The probability that the 50-year-old dies in the next 20 years is

$$P(Y \le 70) = \frac{20}{50} = \frac{2}{5}.$$

(a) $P(X > 65 \text{ and } Y > 70) = \left(1-\frac{4}{11}\right)\left(1-\frac{2}{5}\right) = .3818$

(b) $P(X \le 65 \text{ and } Y \le 70) = \left(\frac{4}{11}\right)\left(\frac{2}{5}\right) = .1455$

8-9. T has an exponential distribution with mean $\frac{1}{\lambda}=500$, or $\lambda=.002$.

$$P(T \le t) = F(t) = 1-e^{-.002t}$$
$$P(T > t) = S(t) = e^{-.002t}$$

(a) $P(T \le 300) = 1-e^{-.002(300)} = 1-e^{-.6} = .4512$

(b) $P(T > 900) = e^{-.002(900)} = e^{-1.8} = .1653$

8-10.   To find the median of the exponential distribution we solve

$$F(t) = 1-e^{-\lambda t} = .50, \text{ or } e^{-\lambda t} = .50.$$

Then $-\lambda t = \ln(.5) = -\ln 2$, and the median is $\left(\frac{1}{\lambda}\right)\ln 2$.

8-11.   For the exponential distribution with mean 60, $\lambda = \frac{1}{60}$.

   (a) $P(T \le 50) = 1 - e^{-.50/.60} = .5654$

   (b) $P(T > 100) = e^{-100/60} = .1889$

8-12.   For the uniform distribution on $[a,b]$,

$$f(t) = \frac{1}{b-a} \text{ and } S(t) = \frac{b-t}{b-a}.$$

   The failure rate is

$$\lambda(t) = \frac{f(t)}{S(t)} = \frac{1}{b-a} \div \frac{b-t}{b-a} = \frac{1}{b-t}.$$

8-13.   Let T be the random variable of the incubation period. T is exponential with $\lambda = \frac{1}{38}$.

   (a) $P(T \le 25) = F(25) = 1 - e^{25/38} = .4821$

   (b) $P(T > 30) = S(30) = e^{-30/38} = .4541$

8-14.   Let T have an exponential distribution with parameter λ. Then $E(T) = 1/\lambda$.

$$F(t) = 1 - e^{-\lambda t}$$
$$F[E(T)] = F(1/\lambda) = 1 - e^{-\lambda(1/\lambda)} = 1 - e^{-1} \approx .632$$

8-15.   Let X and Y be the random variables for the time between accidents at these intersections. Each is exponentially distributed with parameters 2 and 2.5, respectively. Let S_1 and S_2 be their respective survival functions. No accident in a month at an intersection means X (or Y) > 1.

   (a) $P(X > 1 \text{ and } Y > 1) = S_1(1)S_2(1) = (e^{-2})(e^{-2.5}) = .0111$

   (b) $P(X > 1 \text{ or } Y > 1) = S_1(1) + S_2(1) - S_1(1)S_2(1)$
   $= e^{-2} + e^{-2.5} - (e^{-2})(e^{-2.5}) = .2063$

8-16.   If T has an exponential distribution with $\lambda = .15$, then
$F(t) = 1 - e^{-.15t}$. To find t_p, solve $F(t) = p$.

If $p = .25$, $\quad 1 - e^{-.15t} = .25$
$$e^{-.15t} = .75$$
$$-.15t = \ln .75$$
$$t_{.25} = 1.9179$$

If $p = .75$, $\quad 1 - e^{-.15t} = .75$
$$e^{-.15t} = .25$$
$$-.15t = \ln .25$$
$$t_{.75} = 9.2420$$

8-17. $\Gamma(n) = \int_0^\infty x^{n-1} e^{-x} dx \qquad$ (See Equation 8.8)

let $u = x^{n-1}$
$$dv = e^{-x} dx$$
$$du = (n-1)x^{n-2} dx$$
$$v = -e^{-x}$$

$\Gamma(n) = -e^{-x} x^{n-1} \Big|_0^\infty + (n-1) \int_0^\infty x^{n-2} e^{-x} dx$

If $n > 1$, then $-e^{-x} x^{n-1} \Big|_0^\infty = 0$. (See Equation 8.6)

$\Gamma(n) = (n-1) \int_0^\infty x^{(n-1)-1} e^{-x} dx$
$\qquad = (n-1)\Gamma(n-1)$

8-18.   If T is an exponential random variable with parameter λ, then

$$P(T \geq a+b \,|\, T \geq a) = \frac{P(T \geq a+b)}{P(T \geq a)}$$

$$= \frac{e^{-\lambda(a+b)}}{e^{-\lambda a}} = e^{-\lambda b} = P(T \geq b).$$

8-19.   For the population in Exercise 8-11, T (the time until death) was
        exponential with $\lambda = \frac{1}{60}$.

(a) $P(T \le 50 \mid T \ge 40) = 1 - P(T \ge 50 \mid T \ge 40)$
$$= 1 - P(T \ge 10) = 1 - e^{-10/60} = .1535$$

(b) $P(T \ge 100 \mid T \ge 40) = P(T \ge 60) = e^{-60/60} = .3679$

8-20.   For the gamma distribution $f(x) = \frac{\beta^{\alpha}}{\Gamma(\alpha)} x^{\alpha-1} e^{-\beta x}$

and $\int_0^{\infty} x^n e^{-ax} \, dx = \frac{\Gamma(n+1)}{a^{n+1}}$.

$E(X) = \int_0^{\infty} x f(x) \, dx = \frac{\beta^{\alpha}}{\Gamma(\alpha)} \int_0^{\infty} x^{\alpha} e^{-\beta x} \, dx$

$$= \frac{\beta^{\alpha}}{\Gamma(\alpha)} \cdot \frac{\Gamma(\alpha+1)}{\beta^{\alpha+1}} = \frac{\alpha \Gamma(\alpha)}{\beta \Gamma(\alpha)} = \frac{\alpha}{\beta}$$

8-21. $E(X^2) = \int_0^{\infty} x^2 f(x) \, dx$

$$= \frac{\beta^{\alpha}}{\Gamma(\alpha)} \int_0^{\infty} x^{\alpha+1} e^{-\beta x} \, dx$$

$$= \frac{\beta^{\alpha}}{\Gamma(\alpha)} \cdot \frac{\Gamma(\alpha+2)}{\beta^{\alpha+2}} = \frac{(\alpha+1)\Gamma(\alpha+1)}{\Gamma(\alpha)\beta^2} = \frac{(\alpha+1)\alpha}{\beta^2}$$

$V(X) = E(X^2) - E(X)^2 = \frac{\alpha(\alpha+1)}{\beta^2} - \frac{\alpha^2}{\beta^2} = \frac{\alpha}{\beta^2}$

8-22.   If the accidents occur at the rate of 2.5 per month, the waiting
        time between accidents is exponential with $\beta = 2.5$. The waiting
        time from the beginning of observation until the third accident,
        T, has a gamma distribution with $\alpha = 3$ and $\beta = 2.5$.

$$E(T) = \frac{\alpha}{\beta} = \frac{3}{2.5} = 1.2$$

$$V(T) = \frac{\alpha}{\beta^2} = \frac{3}{(2.5)^2} = .48$$

8-23.   The waiting time T until the 12th new employee is hired has a
        gamma distribution with $\alpha = 12$ and $\beta = 8$.

$$E(T) \;=\; \frac{\alpha}{\beta} \;=\; \frac{12}{8} \;=\; 1.5$$

$$V(T) \;=\; \frac{\alpha}{\beta^2} \;=\; \frac{12}{64} \;=\; .1875$$

8-24.   Let T have a gamma distribution with a mean of 18 and a
        variance of 27.

$$\frac{E(T)}{V(T)} \;=\; \frac{\alpha/\beta}{\alpha/\beta^2} \;=\; \beta \;=\; \frac{18}{27} \;=\; \frac{2}{3}$$

$$\alpha \;=\; \beta E(T) \;=\; \left(\tfrac{2}{3}\right)18 \;=\; 12$$

8-25.   Let X have a gamma distribution with $\alpha = 2$ and $\beta = 3$. Then

$$f(x) \;=\; \frac{3^2}{\Gamma(2)} x^{2-1} e^{-3x}.$$

   (a) $F(x) \;=\; 9\displaystyle\int_{0}^{x} t e^{-3t}\, dt$ (integrating by parts)

$$= 9\left(\frac{-t e^{3t}}{3} - \frac{e^{-3t}}{9} \right)\Bigg|_{0}^{x}$$

$$= 1 - e^{-3x}(3x+1)$$

   (b) $P(0 \le X \le 3) \;=\; F(3)$
$$= 1 - e^{-9}(10)$$
$$= .9988$$

   (c) $P(1 \le X \le 2) \;=\; F(2) - F(1)$
$$= (1 - 7e^{-6}) - (1 - 4e^{-3})$$
$$= .1818$$

8-26. X has a gamma distribution with $\alpha = 2$ and $\beta = \frac{1}{3}$.

$$E(X) = 6, \text{ and } E(X^2) = \frac{\alpha(\alpha+1)}{\beta^2} = 54$$

$$
\begin{aligned}
E(C) &= E(500X+5X^2) \\
&= \int_0^\infty (500x+5x^2)f(x)\,dx \\
&= 500\int_0^\infty xf(x)\,dx + 5\int_0^\infty x^2 f(x)\,dx \\
&= 500E(X)+5E(X^2) = 3270
\end{aligned}
$$

8-27.   (a) $F_Z(1.56) - F_Z(-1.15) = .9406 - .1251 = .8155$
         (b) $F_Z(2.13) - F_Z(0.15) = .9834 - .5596 = .4238$
         (c) $F_Z(1.0) - F_Z(-1.0) = .8413 - .1587 = .6826$
         (d) $1 - F_Z(1.65) + F_Z(-1.65) = 1 - .9505 + .0495 = .0990$

8-28.   (a) $F_Z(z) = .8238$, so $z = 0.93$
         (b) $F_Z(z) = .0287$, so $z = -1.90$
         (c) $1 - F_Z(z) = .9115$, so $F_Z(z) = .0885$ and $z = -1.35$
         (d) $1 - F_Z(z) = .1660$, so $F_Z(z) = .8340$ and $z = 0.97$
         (e) By symmetry of the standard normal density function, $P(Z \geq z) = P(Z \leq -z)$.

$$
\begin{aligned}
P(|Z| \geq z) &= P(Z \geq z) + P(Z \leq -z) = 2P(Z \geq z) \\
&= 2\big(1 - F_Z(z)\big) = .10
\end{aligned}
$$

$F_Z(z) = .9500$, so $z = 1.645$

(Note that .9500 falls between two z-values. The z-value of 1.645 is found by interpolation. It is a useful value to know.)

         (f) $P(|Z| \leq z) = 1 - P(|Z| \geq z) = 1 - 2\big(1 - F_Z(z)\big)$

$$= 2F_Z(z) - 1 = .95$$

$F_Z(z) = .9750$, so $z = 1.96$

8-29. Let $Z > 0$ and $F_Z(z) = \alpha = P(Z \le z)$. By symmetry of standard density normal density function:

$$
\begin{aligned}
F_Z(-z) &= P(Z \le -z) \\
&= P(Z \ge z) \\
&= 1 - P(Z \le z) \\
&= 1 - \alpha
\end{aligned}
$$

$$
\begin{aligned}
P(-z \le Z \le z) &= P(Z \le z) - P(Z \le -z) \\
&= \alpha - (1-\alpha) \\
&= 2\alpha - 1
\end{aligned}
$$

In subsequent problems involving probabilities of the normal random variable, the z-values will be rounded to 2 decimal places to make use of the z-table in Appendix A. If you are using the TI-83 or other calculator, this will not be necessary. The solutions here will only be those using the z-table.

8-30. X is a normal random variable with $\mu = 17.1$ and $\sigma = 3.2$.

$$
\begin{aligned}
P(14 \le X \le 25) &= \left(\frac{14 - \mu}{\sigma} \le Z \le \frac{25 - \mu}{\sigma}\right) \\
&= \left(\frac{14 - 17.7}{3.2} \le Z \le \frac{25 - 17.1}{3.2}\right) \\
&= (-.97 \le Z \le 2.47) \\
&= .9932 - .1660 \\
&= .8272
\end{aligned}
$$

8.31 Let S be the total claims on the 5000 policies. Then S has a normal distribution with $\mu = 5000(495)$, $\sigma^2 = 5000(30,000)$, and $\sigma = 12,247.44$.

$$
\begin{aligned}
P(S \le 2,500,000) &= P\left(Z \le \frac{2,500,000 - 2,475,000}{12,247.44}\right) \\
&= P(Z \le 2.04) = .9793
\end{aligned}
$$

8-32.   Let X be the length of the rod. X is normally distributed with mean of 7.505 and standard deviation of .01.

(a) $P(7.48 \le X \le 7.52) = P\left(\dfrac{7.48 - 7.505}{.01} \le Z \le \dfrac{7.52 - 7.505}{.01}\right)$

$$= P(-2.5 \le Z \le 1.5)$$
$$= .9270$$

(b) If 4 rods, let Y be the number that meet the specifications.

$$P(Y \ge 3) = 4(.927)^3(.073) + (.927)^4 = .9711$$

8-33.   Let X be the lifetime of a light bulb, and $\mu = 1500$ and $\sigma = 125$.

(a) $P(X \ge 1400) = P\left(Z \ge \dfrac{1400 - 1500}{125}\right)$

$$= P(Z \ge -.8) = 1 - P(Z \le -.8) = .7881$$

(b) P(all three burning after 1400 hrs) $= (.7881)^3 = .4895$

8-34.   If X is a number picked from $[0,1]$, x is uniformly distributed with mean .5 and variance $\frac{1}{12}$. Let S be the sum of 50 such numbers. Then S is approximately normal with $\mu = 50(.5) = 25$ and $\sigma = \sqrt{50/12} = 2.0412$.

$P(24 \le S \le 27) = P\left(\dfrac{24 - 25}{2.0412} \le Z \le \dfrac{27 - 25}{2.0412}\right)$

$$= P(-.49 \le Z \le .98)$$
$$= .5244$$

8-35. $P(X \le 29.9) = .9192$

$$P\left(Z \le \dfrac{29.9 - 25}{\sigma}\right) = .9192 = F_Z(1.4)$$

$$\dfrac{4.9}{\sigma} = 1.4, \ \sigma = 3.5$$

8-36. Let $Y = e^X$, where X is normal with $\mu = 5$ and $\sigma = .40$.

$$E(Y) = e^{\mu + \frac{\sigma^2}{2}} = e^{5.08} = 160.77$$
$$V(Y) = E(Y)^2(e^{\sigma^2} - 1) = e^{10.16}(e^{.16} - 1) = 4484.96$$

8-37. Let $Y = e^X$, where X is normal with $\mu = 5.2$ and $\sigma = .80$.

$$
\begin{aligned}
P(100 \leq Y \leq 500) &= P(\ln 100 \leq X \leq \ln 500)\\
&= P\left(\frac{\ln 500 - 5.2}{.8} \leq X \leq \frac{\ln 500 - 5.2}{.8}\right)\\
&= P(-.74 \leq X \leq 1.27) = .6684
\end{aligned}
$$

8-38. Let $Y = e^X$, where X is normal with $\mu = 6.8$ and $\sigma = .60$.

$$
\begin{aligned}
P(Y \geq 1750) &= 1 - P(X \leq \ln 1750)\\
&= 1 - P\left(Z \leq \frac{\ln 1750 - 6.8}{.6}\right)\\
&= 1 - P(Z \leq 1.11) = .1335
\end{aligned}
$$

8-39. To find the median of Y we solve the equation

$$P(Y \leq y) = .50$$
$$P(X \leq \ln y) = .50$$
$$P\left(Z \leq \frac{\ln y - \mu}{\sigma}\right) = .50$$
$$\left(\frac{\ln y - \mu}{\sigma}\right) = 0$$
$$\ln y = \mu.$$

Then $y = e^\mu$ is the median.

8-40. $Y = 100e^x$, where X is normal with $\mu = .10$ and $\sigma = .03$.

  (a) $P(100Y \geq 112.50) = 1 - P(100Y \leq 112.5)$

  $$= 1 - P(Y \leq 1.125)$$

  $$= 1 - P(X \leq \ln 1.125)$$

  $$= 1 - P\left(Z \leq \frac{\ln 1.125 - .10}{.03}\right)$$

  $$= 1 - P(Z \leq .59) = .2776$$

  (b) $P(100Y \leq 107.5) = P\left(Z \leq \frac{\ln 1.075 - .1}{.03}\right)$

  $$= P(Z \leq -.92) = .1788$$

8-41.   Let Y be lognormal with $E(Y) = 2500$ and $V(Y) = 1,000,000$.
        Note that $V(Y)$ can be written as

  $$V(Y) = E(Y)^2(e^{\sigma^2} - 1).$$

  $$e^{\sigma^2} - 1 = \frac{1,000,000}{(2500)^2} = 16$$

  $$\sigma^2 = \ln 1.16$$

  $$\sigma = .3853$$

  $$\ln(E(Y)) = \mu + \frac{\sigma^2}{2} = \ln 2500$$

  $$\mu = \ln 2500 - \frac{(.3853)^2}{2} = 7.7498$$

8-42.   Rewrite the Pareto density function as $f(x) = \alpha\beta^\alpha x^{-\alpha-1}$.

  (a) $F(x) = \alpha\beta^\alpha \int_\beta^x t^{-\alpha-1} dt = \alpha\beta^\alpha \frac{t^{-\alpha}}{(-\alpha)}\Big|_\beta^x$

  $$= -\beta^\alpha(x^{-\alpha} - \beta^{-\alpha}) = 1 - \left(\frac{\beta}{x}\right)^\alpha$$

(b) $E(X) = \int_\beta^\infty xf(x)\,dx = \alpha\beta^\alpha \int_\alpha^\infty x^{-\alpha}\,dx$

$$= \frac{\alpha\beta^\alpha}{-\alpha+1} x^{-\alpha+1} \Big|_\beta^\infty$$

$$= \frac{\alpha\beta^\alpha}{-(\alpha-1)}(0 - \beta^{-\alpha+1})$$

$$= \frac{\alpha\beta}{\alpha-1}, \quad (\alpha > 1)$$

(c) $E(X^2) = \int_\beta^\infty x^2 f(x)\,dx = \alpha\beta^\alpha \int_\beta^\infty x^{-\alpha+1}\,dx$

$$= \frac{\alpha\beta^\alpha}{-\alpha+2} x^{-\alpha+2} \Big|_\beta^\infty$$

$$= \frac{\alpha\beta^\alpha}{-(\alpha-2)}(0 - \beta^{-\alpha+2}) = \frac{\alpha\beta^2}{\alpha-2}, \quad (\alpha > 2)$$

$$V(X) = E(X^2) - E(X)^2 = \frac{\alpha\beta^2}{\alpha-2} - \left(\frac{\alpha\beta}{\alpha-1}\right)^2$$

8-43.   Let X be a Pareto random variable with $\alpha = 3.5$ and $\beta = 4$.

(a) $E(X) = \frac{\alpha\beta}{\alpha-1} = \frac{4(3.5)}{2.5} = 5.6$

(b) $V(X) = \frac{\alpha\beta^2}{\alpha-2} - \left[\frac{\alpha\beta}{\alpha-1}\right]^2 = \frac{3.5(16)}{1.5} - 5.6^2 = 5.9733$

(c) To find the median solve $F(x) = 1 - \left(\frac{4}{x}\right)^{3.5} = .50$.

$$\left(\frac{4}{x}\right)^{3.5} = .50$$

$$x = \frac{4}{5^{1/3.5}} = 4.8761$$

(d) $P(6 \le X \le 12) = F(12) - F(6)$

$$= \left[1 - \left(\frac{4}{12}\right)^{3.5}\right] - \left[1 - \left(\frac{4}{6}\right)^{3.5}\right]$$

$$= .97862 - .75808 = .22054$$

8-44.   Because of the deductible, only claims for losses of more than 5
        (hundreds of dollars) are filed. Hence $\beta = 5$. Since the failure
        rate is $\frac{3.5}{x}$, $\alpha = 3.5$.

    (a) Mean loss amount is $E(X) = \frac{(3.5)(5)}{2.5} = 7$.   ($700)

    (b) Expected amount of a single claim is loss – deductible =
        $200.

    (c) $V(100X) = 100^2\left[\frac{(3.5)(25)}{1.5} - 7^2\right] = 93{,}333.33$

8-45.   We are given $\Gamma(1/2) = \pi^{1/2}$, and we know $\Gamma(x+1) = x\Gamma(x)$.

    (a) $\Gamma(3/2) = (1/2)\Gamma(1/2) = (1/2)\pi^{1/2}$

    (b) $\Gamma(5/2) = (3/2)\Gamma(3/2) = (3/4)\pi^{1/2}$

    (c) $\Gamma(7/2) = (5/2)\Gamma(5/2) = (15/8)\pi^{1/2}$

8-46.   For the Weibull distribution $F(x) = 1 - e^{-\beta x^\alpha}$.
        If $\alpha = 3$ and $\beta = 3.5$, then $F(x) = 1 - e^{-3.5x^2}$.

    (a) $P(X \le 0.4) = F(0.4) = 1 - e^{-3.5(.4)^3} = .2007$

    (b) $P(X > 0.8) = 1 - F(0.8) = e^{-3.5(.8)^3} = .1666$

8-47.   The failure rate for the Weibull distribution is $\lambda(x) = \alpha\beta x^{\alpha-1}$.

        If $\alpha = 3$ and $\beta = 3.5$, then $\lambda(x) = 10.5x^2$.

8-48.   Let X be a Weibull distribution with $\alpha = 2$ and $\beta = 3.5$.

(a) $E(X) = \dfrac{\Gamma\left(1+\frac{1}{\alpha}\right)}{\beta^{1/\alpha}} = \dfrac{\Gamma\left(\frac{3}{2}\right)}{\sqrt{3.5}} = \dfrac{\left(\frac{1}{2}\right)\pi^{1/2}}{\sqrt{3.5}} = .4737$

(b) $V(X) = \dfrac{1}{\beta^{2/\alpha}}\left[\Gamma\left(1+\frac{2}{\alpha}\right)-\Gamma\left(1+\frac{1}{\alpha}\right)^2\right]$

$= \left(\dfrac{1}{3.5}\right)\left[\Gamma(2)-\Gamma\left(\frac{3}{2}\right)^2\right]$

$= \left(\dfrac{1}{3.5}\right)\left(1-\frac{\pi}{4}\right) = .0613$

(c) $P(.25 \le X \le .75) = (1-e^{-3.5(.75)^2})-(1-e^{-3.5(.25)^2})$

$= (1-.13963)-(1-.80352) = .66389$

8-49.   The Weibull density function is $f(x) = \alpha\beta x^{\alpha-1}e^{-\beta x^\alpha}$.

$$E(X) = \int_0^\infty xf(x)\,dx = \alpha\beta \int_0^\infty x^\alpha e^{-\beta x^\alpha}\,dx$$

Let $\quad \mu = x^\alpha \quad\quad x = \mu^{1/\alpha} \quad\quad dx = \left(\frac{1}{\alpha}\right)\mu^{1/\alpha-1}\,du$

$x^\alpha e^{-\beta x^\alpha}\,dx = ue^{-\beta u}\left(\frac{1}{\alpha}\right)u^{1/\alpha-1}\,du = \left(\frac{1}{\alpha}\right)u^{1/\alpha}e^{-\beta u}\,du$

$E(X) = \alpha\beta\int_0^\infty \left(\frac{1}{\alpha}\right)u^{1/\alpha}e^{-\beta u}\,du = \beta\dfrac{\Gamma\left(1+\frac{1}{\alpha}\right)}{\beta^{1/\alpha+1}} = \dfrac{\Gamma\left(1+\frac{1}{\alpha}\right)}{\beta^{1/\alpha}}$

8-50.   Let X be a beta distribution with $\alpha = 4$ and $\beta = 1.5$.

$f(x) = \dfrac{\Gamma(\alpha+\beta)}{\Gamma(\alpha)\Gamma(\beta)}x^{\alpha-1}(1-x)^{\beta-1}$

$= \dfrac{\Gamma(5.5)}{\Gamma(4)\Gamma(1.5)}x^3(1-x)^{.5}$

$= \dfrac{\left(\frac{9}{2}\right)\left(\frac{7}{2}\right)\left(\frac{5}{2}\right)\left(\frac{3}{2}\right)\Gamma\left(\frac{3}{2}\right)}{(3!)\Gamma\left(\frac{3}{2}\right)}x^3(1-x)^{.5} = 315x^3\dfrac{(1-x)^{1/2}}{32}$

8-51.   We need to find k so that $\int_0^1 kx^4(1-x)^2\, dx\ =\ 1.$

$$\int_0^1(x^4-2x^5+x^6)\,dx\ =\ \left(\tfrac{x^5}{5}-\tfrac{2x^6}{6}+\tfrac{x^7}{7}\right)\Big|_0^1$$

$$=\ \tfrac{1}{5}-\tfrac{1}{3}+\tfrac{1}{7}\ =\ \tfrac{1}{105}$$

Hence $k = 105.$

8-52.   For the beta distribution with $\alpha = 3$ and $\beta = 2$:

$$E(X)\ =\ \tfrac{\alpha}{\alpha+\beta}\ =\ \tfrac{3}{6}\ =\ 0.6$$

$$V(X)\ =\ \frac{\alpha\beta}{(\alpha+\beta)^2(\alpha+\beta+1)}\ =\ \frac{6}{25(6)}\ =\ 0.04$$

8-53. $P(X \le 0.5)\ =\ \dfrac{\Gamma(5)}{\Gamma(3)\Gamma(2)}\displaystyle\int_0^{.5} x^2(1-x)\,dx$

$$=\ 12\int_0^{.5}(x^2-x^3)\,dx$$

$$=\ 12\left(\tfrac{x^3}{3}-\tfrac{x^4}{4}\right)\Big|_0^{.5}\ =\ 12\left[\left(\tfrac{1}{3}\right)(.5)^3-\left(\tfrac{1}{4}\right)(.5)^4\right]=.3125$$

8-54.   For a beta distribution with $\alpha = 2$ and $\beta = 4$:

$$P(X \le 0.3)\ =\ \dfrac{\Gamma(6)}{\Gamma(2)\Gamma(4)}\displaystyle\int_0^{.3} x(1-x)^3\,dx$$

$$=\ 20\int_0^{.3}(x-3x^2+3x^3-x^4)\,dx$$

$$=\ 20\left(\tfrac{x^2}{2}-x^3+\tfrac{3x^4}{4}-\tfrac{x^5}{5}\right)\Big|_0^{.3}$$

$$=\ 30\left[\left(\tfrac{1}{2}\right)(.3)^2-(.3)^3+\left(\tfrac{3}{4}\right)(.3)^4-\left(\tfrac{1}{5}\right)(.3)^5\right]$$

$$=\ .47178$$

8-55. Let X have a beta distribution with parameters α and β.

$$E(X) = \int_0^1 x f(x)\, dx = \frac{\Gamma(\alpha+\beta)}{\Gamma(\alpha)\Gamma(\beta)} \int_0^1 x^\alpha (1-x)^{\beta-1}\, dx$$

(and using Equation 8.33)

$$= \frac{\Gamma(\alpha+\beta)}{\Gamma(\alpha)\Gamma(\beta)} \cdot \frac{\Gamma(\alpha+1)\Gamma(\beta)}{\Gamma(\alpha+\beta+1)} = \frac{\alpha}{\alpha+\beta}$$

8-56. Let X be the time until failure of the device. We are asked to find
$P(X \geq 5) = 1 - F(5)$.

We are not given the parameter λ for the exponential, but we
can use the given information about the median to find it. The
cumulative distribution for the exponential is $F(x) = 1 - e^{-\lambda x}$.
By definition of the median m,

$$F(m) = .50.$$

Since $m = 4$ we have

$$F(m) = F(4) = 1 - e^{-\lambda 4} = .50$$

$$e^{-\lambda 4} = .50 \qquad \rightarrow \qquad \lambda = \frac{\ln(.50)}{-4} = .17329$$

Thus

$$P(X \geq 5) = 1 - F(5) = e^{-5\lambda} = .42045$$

Note that this problem goes easily if you have F(x) memorized.

8-57.   Recall that the mean of the exponential is $\mu = \frac{1}{\lambda}$. Thus if you are

given the mean (as in this problem), you know that $\frac{1}{\mu} = \lambda$. Let G

be the waiting time for the first accident for a good driver and B
be the waiting time for the first accident for a bad driver. Then λ
and the cumulative distribution function for G and B are:

G: $\lambda_G = \frac{1}{6}$ $F_G(x) = \left(1 - e^{-x/6}\right)$

B: $\lambda_B = \frac{1}{3}$ $F_B(x) = \left(1 - e^{-x/3}\right)$

We are asked to find $P(G \le 3 \ \& \ B \le 2)$. We are given that G and
B are independent. Thus

$$
\begin{aligned}
P(G \le 3 \ \& \ B \le 2) &= P(G \le 3)P(B \le 2) \\
&= F_G(3)F_B(2) \\
&= (1 - e^{-3/6})(1 - e^{-2/3}) \\
&= 1 - e^{-2/3} - e^{-1/2} + e^{-7/6} \approx .1915
\end{aligned}
$$

Note again how important it is to know $F(x)$.

8-58.   We will look at a single printer first. Let X_i be the amount of the
refund on printer i and T_i the lifetime (time to failure) of printer i.
T_i is exponential with $\mu = 2$ and $\lambda = \frac{1}{2}$. Thus $F_T(x) = 1 - e^{-x/2}$.
The probabilities of the possible refund amounts are

$$
\begin{aligned}
P(X_i = 200) = P(0 \le T_i \le 1) &= F(1) \\
&= 1 - e^{-1/2} = .39347
\end{aligned}
$$

$$
\begin{aligned}
P(X_i = 100) = P(1 < T_i \le 2) &= F(2) - F(1) \\
&= 1 - e^{-2/2} - (1 - e^{-1/2}) = .23865
\end{aligned}
$$

Then

$$
E(X_i) = 200(.39347) + 100(.23865) = 102.56.
$$

The total amount paid is $S = X_1 + \cdots + X_{100}$. The expected
amount paid is

$$
E(S) = E(X_1 + \cdots + X_{100}) = 100E(X_i) = 10,256.
$$

8-59. Let T be the time in days until the first accident for a high-risk driver. We are asked to find

$$P(T \le 80) = F(80).$$

We know that $F(t) = 1 - e^{-\lambda t}$ but we do not know λ. That can be found using the other given information.

$$.30 = P(T \le 50) = F(50). = 1 - e^{-50\lambda}$$

$$e^{-50\lambda} = .70 \quad \rightarrow \quad \lambda = \frac{\ln(.70)}{-50} = .0071335$$

Now we have λ and can finish the problem.

$$P(T \le 80) = F(80) = 1 - e^{-80\lambda} = .4348$$

8-60. You can see by direct examination that X must be exponential with $c = .004$, since $.004e^{-0.004x}$ is the density function for the exponential with $\lambda = .004$. (Some of our students integrated the density function and set the total area under the curve equal to 1, but that takes extra time.) For the original expense X the cumulative distribution function is $F(x) = 1 - e^{-.004x}$. Thus the median m for X is obtained by solving the equation

$$F(m) = 0.50 = 1 - e^{-.004m}$$

$$0.50 = e^{-.004m}$$

$$m = \frac{\ln(.50)}{-.004} = 173.3$$

The actual benefit is not exactly the same as the original loss random variable X, since claim payments are capped at 250. Since 173.3 is less than 250, 50% of the benefits paid are still less than 173.3 and 50% are greater.

8-61.   There are no claims when $N = 0$, and thus S must be 0 in this case. We will break down $P(4 < S < 8)$ into two cases depending on whether $N = 1$ or $N > 1$.

$$
\begin{aligned}
P(4 < S < 8) &= P\big[(N = 1 \,\&\, 4 < S < 8) \text{ or } (N > 1 \,\&\, 4 < S < 8)\big] \\
&= P(N = 1 \,\&\, 4 < S < 8) + P(N > 1 \,\&\, 4 < S < 8) \\
&= P(4 < S < 8 \mid N = 1)P(N = 1) \\
&\qquad + P(4 < S < 8 \mid N > 1)P(N > 1) \\
&= P(4 < S < 8 \mid N = 1)\tfrac{1}{3} + P(4 < S < 8 \mid N > 1)\tfrac{1}{6}
\end{aligned}
$$

When $N = 1$, $\mu = 5$ and $\lambda = \tfrac{1}{5}$. Thus $F(x) = 1 - e^{-x/5}$. This gives us

$$
P(4 < S < 8 \mid N = 1) = F(8) - F(4) = e^{-4/5} - e^{-8/5} = .24743
$$

When $N > 1$, $\mu = 8$ and $\lambda = \tfrac{1}{8}$. Thus $F(x) = 1 - e^{-x/8}$. This gives us

$$
P(4 < S < 8 \mid N > 1) = F(8) - F(4) = e^{-4/8} - e^{-8/8} = .23865
$$

Thus

$$
\begin{aligned}
P(4 < S < 8) &= P(4 < S < 8 \mid N = 1)\tfrac{1}{3} + P(4 < S < 8 \mid N > 1)\tfrac{1}{6} \\
&= (.24743)\tfrac{1}{3} + (.23865)\tfrac{1}{6} = .122
\end{aligned}
$$

8-62.   Let X_i be the number of claims on policy i, $i = 1, \ldots, 1250$. The Poisson random variables X_i are iid with mean $\mu = 2$ and variance $\sigma^2 = 2$. The total number of claims is

$$
S = X_1 + \cdots + X_{1250}.
$$

By the central limit theorem, S is approximately normal with

$$
E(S) = \mu_s = 1250(2) = 2500
$$

$$
V(S) = \sigma_s^2 = 1250(2) = 2500
$$

$$
\sigma_S = \sqrt{2500} = 50
$$

Thus

$$P(2450 \le S \le 2600) = P\left(\frac{2450-2500}{50} \le Z \le \frac{2600-2500}{50}\right)$$
$$= P(-1 \le Z \le 2) = .3413 + .4772 = .8185$$

8-63   Let X_i be the claim amount on policy i, $i = 1,...,100$. The exponential random variables X_i are iid with mean $\mu = 1000$ and variance $\sigma^2 = 1000^2$. Then the premium for each single policy is $\pi = 1000 + 100 = 1100$, 100 over the expected claim amount. Total premiums collected are $100(1100) = 110,000$.

The total claim amount is

$$S = X_1 + \cdots + X_{100}.$$

By the central limit theorem, S is approximately normal with

$$E(S) = \mu_s = 100(1000) = 100,000$$
$$V(S) = \sigma_s^2 = 100(1000)^2$$
$$\sigma_S = \sqrt{100(1000)^2} = 10,000$$

Thus the probability that claims exceed premiums is

$$P(S \ge 110,000) = P\left(Z \ge \frac{110,000-100,000}{10,000}\right)$$
$$= P(Z \ge 1) = 1 - .8413 = .1587$$

8-64.   We will first look at one recruit. Let X_i be the number of pensions that recruit i will have. There can be 0, 1 or 2 pensions. We find their probabilities next.

0 pensions
$P(0 \text{ pensions}) = P(\text{recruit does not remain}) = 1 - .4 = .6$

1 pension
$P(1 \text{ pension}) = P(\text{recruit remains and is not married at retirement})$
$= P(\text{remain})P(\text{not married}|\text{remain}) = .40(.25) = .10$

2 pensions
$P(2 \text{ pension})P(\text{recruit remains and is married at retirement})$
$= P(\text{remain})P(\text{married}|\text{remain}) = .40(.75) = .30$

Thus

$$E(X) = 0(.6)+1(.1)+2(.3) = .7$$
$$E(X^2) = 0^2(.6)+1^2(.1)+2^2(.3) = 1.3$$

$$V(X) = 1.3-.7^2 = .81 \qquad \sigma_X = \sqrt{.81} = .9$$

The random variables X_i are iid. The total number of pensions is

$$S = X_1 + \cdots + X_{100},$$

with

$$E(S) = \mu_s = 100(.7) = 70,$$
$$V(S) = \sigma_s^2 = 100(.81) = 81$$

and

$$\sigma_S = \sqrt{81} = 9.$$

In this problem we will use the continuity correction. The probability of at most 90 pensions is

$$P(S \le 90.5) = P\left(Z \le \frac{90.5-70}{9}\right) = P(Z \le 2.28) = .9887$$

Note: If you had not used the continuity correction you still would have gotten a probability of .9869 and the same final answer.

8-65.   We will first look at the difference between true age and rounded age for one individual. Let X_i be the difference between true and rounded age for person i. We are told that X_i is uniform on the interval $[-2.5, 2.5]$. Thus

$$E(X_i) = \frac{-2.5+2.5}{2} = 0$$
$$V(X_i) = \frac{(2.5-(-2.5))^2}{12} = 2.0833.$$

We are asked to find the probability that the mean difference for the 48 individuals is within .25 years of the true mean difference, which is $E(X_i) = 0$. The mean difference for the 48 individuals is

$$\overline{X} = \frac{X_1 + \cdots + X_{48}}{48}.$$

We really need to find $P(-.25 \le \overline{X} \le .25)$. Since n is large, the sample mean $\overline{X}$ will be approximately normal with $\mu = 0$, variance $\frac{\sigma^2}{n} = \frac{2.0833}{48} = .0434$ and standard deviation $\sqrt{.0434} = .20833$.

$$P(-.25 \le \overline{X} \le .25) = P\left(\frac{-.25 - 0}{.20833} \le Z \le \frac{.25 - 0}{.20833}\right)$$
$$= P(-1.20 \le Z \le 1.20) = .7698$$

8-66.   Let X_i be the amount of contribution i, $i = 1,\ldots,2025$. The random variables X_i are iid with mean $\mu = 3125$ and variance $\sigma^2 = 250^2$. The total contribution is

$$S = X_1 + \cdots + X_{2025}.$$

By the central limit theorem, S is approximately normal with

$$E(S) = \mu_s = 3125(2025) = 6{,}328{,}125$$
$$V(S) = \sigma_s^2 = 250^2(2025) = 126{,}562{,}500$$
$$\sigma_S = \sqrt{126{,}562{,}600} = 11{,}250$$

Since $z_{.90} = 1.282$, the 90th percentile of S is

$$s_{.90} = 6{,}328{,}125 + 1.282(11{,}250) = 6{,}342{,}547.5$$

CHAPTER 9

9-1. With a deductible of $300, the claim amount is $g(x) = x - 300$, for $x \geq 300$, and 0 elsewhere.

$$E[g(X)] = \int_0^\infty g(x)(.001e^{-.001x})\, dx$$

$$= \int_{300}^\infty (x-300)(.001e^{-.001x})\, dx$$

$$= \int_{300}^\infty x(.001e^{-.001x})\, dx - 300 \int_{300}^\infty (.001e^{-.001x})\, dx$$

(the first integral uses integration by parts)

$$= \left(\left[(-xe^{.001x} - 1000e^{-.001x}) + 300e^{-.001x} \right] \right]_{300}^\infty$$

$$= (-x - 700)e^{-.001x} \Big|_{300}^\infty$$

$$= 1000e^{-3} = 740.82$$

9-2. If the policy in Exercise 9-1 also has a payment cap of $1500, then

$$h(x) = \begin{cases} 0, 0 < x < 300 \\ x - 300, 300 \leq x \leq 1800. \\ 1500, x > 1800 \end{cases}$$

$$E[h(X)] = \int_0^\infty h(x)(.001e^{-.001x})\, dx$$

$$= \int_{300}^{1800} (x-300)(.001e^{-.001x})\, dx$$

$$+ \int_{1800}^\infty 1500(.001e^{-.001x})\, dx$$

$$= \left[(-x-700)e^{-.001x} \right]_{300}^{1800} - 1500e^{-.001x} \Big|_{1800}^\infty$$

$$= -2500e^{-1.8} + 1000e^{-3} + 1500e^{-1.8} = 575.52$$

9-3. Using the utility function $u(w) = \ln(w)$, the expected utilities are as follows:

Method 1: W_1 is uniformly distributed over $[9,11]$, so $f(x) = \frac{1}{2}$ for $9 \le w \le 11$.

$$
\begin{aligned}
E[u(W_1)] &= \int_9^{11} \left(\tfrac{1}{2}\right)\ln(w)\, dw \\
&= \left(\tfrac{1}{2}\right)[w\ln(w) - w]\Big|_9^{11} \\
&= \left(\tfrac{1}{2}\right)(11\ln 11 - 9\ln 9 - 2) = 2.3009
\end{aligned}
$$

Method 2: W_2 is uniformly distributed over $[5,15]$, so $f(x) = \frac{1}{10}$ for $5 \le w \le 15$.

$$
\begin{aligned}
E[u(W_2)] &= \int_5^{15} \left(\tfrac{1}{10}\right)\ln(w)\, dw \\
&= \left(\tfrac{1}{10}\right)[w\ln(w) - w]\Big|_5^{15} \\
&= \left(\tfrac{1}{10}\right)(15\ln 15 - 5\ln 5 - 10) = 2.2574
\end{aligned}
$$

Hence Method 1 has higher expected utility and should be chosen.

9-4. If X is uniformly distributed over $[a,b]$, then $f(x) = \frac{1}{b-a}$.

$$
M_X(t) = E[e^{tX}] = \frac{1}{b-a}\int_a^b e^{tx}\, dx = \frac{e^{tx}}{t(b-a)}\Big|_a^b = \frac{e^{bt} - e^{at}}{t(b-a)}
$$

9-5. For the moment generating function in Exercise 9-4,

$$
M'_X(t) = \frac{t(be^{bt} - ae^{at}) - (e^{bt} - e^{at})}{(b-a)t^2}.
$$

As t approaches 0, the expression assumes an indeterminate form, so we must use L'Hospital's rule.

$$
\begin{aligned}
M'_X(0) &= \lim_{t \to 0} \frac{(be^{bt} - ae^{at}) + t(b^2 e^{bt} - a^2 e^{at}) - (be^{bt} + ae^{at})}{2t(b-a)} \\
&= \lim_{t \to 0} \frac{b^2 e^{bt} - a^2 e^{at}}{2(b-a)} = \frac{b^2 - a^2}{2(b-a)} = \frac{a+b}{2} = E[X]
\end{aligned}
$$

Note that in the case of the uniform distribution, it is inefficient to find moments using $M_X(t)$.

9-6.   If $f(x) = 2(1-x)$ for $0 \le x \le 1$ and 0 elsewhere, then

$$M_X(t) = E[e^{tX}] = \int_0^1 e^{tx} 2(1-x)\, dx$$

$$= 2\int_0^1 e^{tx}\, dx - 2\int_0^1 xe^{tx}\, dx$$

$$= 2\left(\frac{e^{tx}}{t} - \frac{xe^{tx}}{t} + \frac{e^{tx}}{t^2}\right)\Big|_0^1$$

$$= \frac{2e^t - 2t - 2}{t^2}, \quad \text{for } t \ne 0, \text{ and } 1 \text{ if } t = 0.$$

9-7.   For the moment generating function in Exercise 9-6,

$$M_X'(t) = \frac{t^2(2e^t - 2) - 2t(2e^t - 2t - 2)}{t^4} = \frac{2te^t - 4e^t + 2t + 4}{t^3}.$$

As t approaches 0, the expression assumes an indeterminate form, so we must use L'Hospitals's rule.

$$M_X'(0) = \lim_{t \to 0} \frac{2te^t - 2e^t + 2}{3t^2} = \lim_{t \to 0} \frac{2te^t}{6t} = \frac{1}{3} = E(X).$$

9-8.   The moment generating function for the gamma distribution with parameters α and β is

$$M_X(t) = \left(\frac{\beta}{\beta - t}\right)^\alpha.$$

Thus $\left(\frac{2}{2-t}\right)^5$ is the moment generating function for the gamma distribution with $\alpha = 5$ and $\beta = 2$.

9-9.   The moment generating function for the exponential distribution with $\lambda = 3$ is

$$M_X(t) = \left(\frac{3}{3-t}\right),$$

so

$$M_{2X+5}(t) = e^{5t} M_X(2t) = e^{5t}\left(\frac{3}{3-2t}\right).$$

9-10.   Let X be the random variable with moment generating function

$$M_X(t) = e^{t+t^2}$$

$$M'_X(t) = (1+2t)e^{t+t^2}$$

$$M'_X(0) = 1 = E(X)$$

$$M''_X(t) = (1+2t)^2 e^{t+t^2} + 2e^{t+t^2}$$

$$M''_X(0) = 1+2 = 3 = E(X^2)$$

$$V(X) = E(X^2) - E(X)^2 = 2$$

9-11.   For the normal distribution, $M_X(t) = e^{\mu t + (\sigma^2 t^2)/2}$.

$$M'_X(t) = (\mu+\sigma^2 t)M_X(t)$$

$$M''_X(t) = (\mu+\sigma^2 t)^2 M_X(t) + \sigma^2 M_X(t)$$

$$M''_X(0) = \mu^2 + \sigma^2 = E(X^2). \quad \left(\text{Re}\,call\ M_X(0) = 1\right)$$

$$V(X) = E(X^2) - E(X)^2 = \mu^2 + \sigma^2 - \mu^2 = \sigma^2$$

9-12.   If X is uniformly distributed over $[0,1]$, then $F(x) = x, \ 0 \le x \le 1$.
If $Y = e^X = g(X)$, then $X = \ln Y = h(Y)$. Since $0 \le x \le 1$, then
$1 \le e^x \le e$.

(a) $F_Y(y) = F_X[h(y)] = \ln y, \text{ for } 1 \le y \le e$

(b) $f_Y(y) = F'_Y(y) = \frac{d}{dy}\ln y = \frac{1}{y}, \text{ for } 1 \le y \le e$

9-13.   If $f_X(x) = 3x^{-4}$, then $F_X(x) = 1 - x^{-3}$ for $x \geq 1$.

If $y = g(x) = \ln x$, then $x = h(y) = e^y$ for $y \geq 0$.

$$F_Y(y) = F_X[h(y)] = 1 - (e^y)^{-3} = 1 - e^{-3y}, \quad \text{for } y \geq 0.$$

9-14.   If $f_X(x) = 3x^{-4}$ then $F_X(x) = 1 - x^{-3}$ and $S_X = x^{-3}$ for $x \geq 1$.

If $y = g(x) = \frac{1}{x}$, then $x = h(y) = \frac{1}{y}$ for $0 < y < 1$. Note that $g(x)$ is strictly decreasing for $x \geq 1$.

(a) $F_Y(y) = S_X[h(y)] = \left(\frac{1}{y}\right)^{-3} = y^3$, for $0 < y < 1$

(b) $f_Y(y) = F_Y'(y) = 3y^2$, for $0 < y \leq 1$

9-15.   Let X be exponentially distributed with unknown parameter λ, and let $P(X > 100) = e^{-100\lambda} = .64$. Let $Y = 2X$.

$$P(X>100) = P(2X>100)$$
$$= P(X>50)$$
$$= e^{-50\lambda}$$
$$= \sqrt{.64}$$
$$= .80.$$

9-16. $P[F(x) \leq x] = P\left[X \leq F^{-1}(x)\right]$
$$= F\left[F^{-1}(x)\right]$$
$$= x$$

The table below gives random numbers used to simulate $F(x)$ in Exercises 9-17 and 9-18. The second and third columns give the transformed values $x = F^{-1}(u)$ for the distributions in 9-17 and 9-18, respectively.

Trial	Random No. (u)	$F^{-1}(u) = 4u$	$F^{-1}(u) = \dfrac{3}{\sqrt[3]{1-u}}$
1	.90643	3.6257	6.6081
2	.17842	0.7137	3.2031
3	.55660	2.2264	3.9342
4	.55071	2.2028	3.9169
5	.96216	3.8486	8.9359
6	.81008	3.2403	5.2191
7	.49660	1.9864	3.7712
8	.92602	3.7041	7.1463
9	.71729	2.8692	4.5710
10	.39443	1.5777	3.5460
11	.15533	0.6213	3.1736
12	.29701	1.1880	3.3739
13	.82751	3.3100	5.3893
14	.67490	2.6996	4.3630
15	.68556	2.7422	4.4117
16	.31329	1.2532	3.4004
17	.68995	2.7598	4.4325
18	.77787	3.1115	4.9536
19	.66928	2.6771	4.3381
20	.53100	2.1240	3.8613

9-17.   If X is uniformly distributed over $[0,4]$ then $u = F(x) = x/4$, for $0 \le x \le 4$. So $x = F^{-1}(u) = 4u$, for $0 \le u \le 1$. Using the above table you can count the number of values of x in each subinterval. Answer 2, 4, 8 and 6 in the respective intervals.

9-18.   If X has a Pareto distribution with $\alpha = 3$ and $\beta = 3$, then $u = F(x) = 1-\left(\frac{3}{x}\right)^3$, for $x \ge 3$. So $x = F^{-1}(u) = \dfrac{3}{\sqrt[3]{1-u}}$, for $0 \le u < 1$. Using the above table you count the number of values in each subinterval. Answer 9, 6, 2 and 3 in the respective intervals.

9-19. Let S be the event that a minor claim is made, and L be the event that a major claim is made. Then

$$P(S) = .09 \text{ and } P(L) = .01.$$

Case 1: $x = 0$

This represents those who filed no claims, so $F(0) = .90$.

Case 2: $0 < x \le 1000$

Since 9 percent filed minor claims and these claims are uniformly distributed over this range,

$$P(X \le x) = P(0) + P(0 < X \le 1000)P(S)$$
$$= .90 + .09\left(\frac{x}{1000}\right).$$

Case 3: $1000 < x \le 10,000$

Since 1 percent filed major claims and these claims are uniformly distributed over this range,

$$P(X \le x) = P(X \le 1000) + P(1000 < X \le 10,000)P(L)$$
$$= .99 + .01\frac{x - 1000}{9000}.$$

9-20. For the policy in Exercise 9-19, $f(x) = \frac{.09}{1000}$, for $0 < x \le 1000$, and $f(x) = \frac{.01}{9000}$, $1000 < x \le 10,000$.

$$E(X) = \int_0^{1000} x\left(\frac{.09}{1000}\right) dx + \int_{1000}^{10,000} x\left(\frac{.01}{9000}\right) dx$$
$$= \frac{.09}{1000}\left(\frac{x^2}{2}\right)\Big|_0^{1,000} + \frac{.01}{9000}\left(\frac{x^2}{2}\right)\Big|_{1,000}^{10,000}$$
$$= 45 + 55 = 100$$

9-21.   Let S be the event that a claim is filed. $P(S) = .10$. Let Y be the random variable for the amount of the claim filed. Y has a Pareto distribution with $\alpha = 3$ and $\beta = 200$.

$$P(Y \le y) = 1 - \left(\frac{200}{y}\right)^3 \text{ for } y > 200$$

Let X be the random variable of the amount paid, $X = y - 200$.

$$P(X \le x \mid S) = 1 - \left(\frac{200}{200 + x}\right)^3, \text{ for } x > 0$$

Case 1: $x = 0$
      No claim is filed, so $F(0) = .90$.

Case 2: $x > 0$
$$P(X \le x) = P(X=0) + P(0 \le X \le x \mid S)P(S)$$
$$= .90 + .10\left[1 - \left(\frac{200}{200+x}\right)^3\right]$$

9-22.   The survival function $S(x) = e^{-\int_0^x \lambda(t)\,dt}$. If $\lambda(t) = \frac{2}{1+x}$, then

$$\int_0^x \frac{2}{1+t}\,dt = 2\ln(1+x) = \ln(1+x)^2.$$
$$e^{-2\ln(1+x)} = \frac{1}{(1+x)^2} = S(x), \text{ for } x \ge 0$$

9-23.   If the hazard rate is $\lambda(x) = \frac{1}{100 - x}$, for $0 \le x < 100$, then

$$-\int_0^x \frac{1}{100 - t}\,dt = \ln(100 - t)\big|_0^x.$$
$$= \ln(100 - x) - \ln(100) = \ln\left(\frac{100 - x}{100}\right).$$
$$S(x) = \frac{100 - x}{100}, \text{ for } 0 \le x < 100$$

9-24.   If $S(x) = \frac{1}{(1+x)^2}$, for $x \ge 0$, then

$$E(X) = \int_0^\infty S(x)\,dx = \int_0^\infty \frac{1}{(1+x)^2}\,dx = \frac{-1}{1+x}\Big|_0^\infty = 1.$$

9-25. If $S(x) = \frac{100-x}{100}$, for $0 \le x < 100$, then

$$E(x) \;=\; \int_0^{100} \frac{100-x}{100}\,dx \;=\; -\frac{(100-x)^2}{200}\Big|_0^{100} \;=\; 50.$$

9-26. The amount paid $g(X)$ is given by

$$g(X) \;=\; \begin{cases} 0 & \text{for } X \le C \\ X - C & \text{otherwise} \end{cases}$$

Thus the probability that the insurance payment is less than 0.5 is equal to $P(X < C+.5)$, and this is equal to .64. If follows that

$$P(X < C+.5) \;=\; .64$$
$$= \int_0^{C+.5} 2x\,dx \;=\; (C+.5)^2$$
$$C + .5 \;=\; .8$$
$$C \;=\; .3$$

9-27. Let X be the random variable for the actual loss, and Y be the random variable for the part of the loss not paid by the insurance policy. We need to find $E(Y)$. Since there is a deductible of 2,

$$Y \;=\; \begin{cases} x, & .6 < x < 2 \\ 2, & x \ge 2 \end{cases}.$$

$$E(Y) \;=\; \int_{.6}^{2} x\left(\frac{2.5(0.6)^{2.5}}{x^{3.5}}\right)dx \;+\; \int_{2}^{\infty} 2\left(\frac{2.5(0.6)^{2.5}}{x^{3.5}}\right)dx$$
$$= \frac{2.5(0.6)^{2.5}x^{-1.5}}{-1.5}\Big|_{.6}^{2} + \frac{5(0.6)^{2.5}x^{-2.5}}{-2.5}\Big|_{2}^{\infty}$$
$$= .83568 + .09859$$
$$= .93427$$

9-28.   Let d denote the unknown deductible and Y denote the amount paid by the insurance. We must first find expressions for Y and $E(Y)$ in terms of the unknown deductible d.

$$Y = \begin{cases} 0, & x < d \\ x - d, & x \geq d \end{cases}$$

The density function for X is $f(x) = \frac{1}{1000}$, $0 \leq x \leq 1000$. Thus

$$E(Y) = \int_0^d 0 \left(\frac{1}{1000}\right) dx + \int_d^{1000} (x-d)\left(\frac{1}{1000}\right) dx$$
$$= \frac{(x-d)^2}{2000}\Big|_d^{1000} = \frac{(1000-d)^2}{2000}$$

We are asked to find d such that $E(Y) = .25E(X)$. For the uniform X on $[0,1000]$, $E(X) = 500$ and $.25E(X) = 125$. Thus we have:

$$E(Y) = .25E(X)$$

$$\frac{(1000-d)^2}{2000} = 125$$

$$(1000-d)^2 = 250,000$$

$$d = 500$$

9-29.   Let T be the random variable for the lifetime (time to failure) of the piece of equipment and Y the random variable for the amount paid by the insurance.

$$Y = \begin{cases} x, & 0 \leq t \leq 1 \\ .5x, & 1 < t \leq 3 \\ 0, & \text{otherwise} \end{cases}$$

The density function for T is $f(t) = \frac{e^{-t/10}}{10}$. We can find $E(Y)$, but it will have the unknown amount x in it.

$$E(Y) = \int_0^1 x\left(\frac{e^{-t/10}}{10}\right)dt + \int_1^3 .5x\left(\frac{e^{-t/10}}{10}\right)dt$$

$$= -xe^{-t/10}\Big|_0^1 - .5xe^{-t/10}\Big|_1^3$$

$$= .09516x + .09201x = .17717x$$

We need this expected payment to equal 1000.

$$.17717x = 1000$$
$$x = 5644.30$$

9-30.   The density function for T is $f(t) = \frac{e^{-t/3}}{3}$. The random variable $X = \max(T, 2)$ can be written as

$$X = \begin{cases} 2, & 0 \le t \le 2 \\ t, & 2 \le t \end{cases}$$

$$E(X) = \int_0^2 2\left(\frac{e^{-t/3}}{3}\right)dt + \int_2^\infty t\left(\frac{e^{-t/3}}{3}\right)dt$$

$$= -2e^{-t/3}\Big|_0^2 + (-te^{-t/3} - 3e^{-t/3})\Big|_2^\infty$$

$$= 2[1 - e^{-2/3}] + 0 + 5e^{-2/3} = 2 + 3e^{-2/3}$$

Note: This problem illustrates the need to be able to do integration by parts on Exam P.

9-31.   Let B denote the random variable for the benefit paid.

$$B = \begin{cases} y, & 1 < y < 10 \\ 10, & 10 \le y \end{cases}$$

$$E(B) = \int_1^{10} y\left(\frac{2}{y^3}\right)dy + \int_{10}^\infty 10\left(\frac{2}{y^3}\right)dt$$

$$= -2y^{-1}\Big|_1^{10} - 10y^{-2}\Big|_{10}^\infty$$

$$= 2\left[1 - \tfrac{1}{10}\right] - 10\left[0 - \tfrac{1}{100}\right] = 1.9$$

9-32. Y can be expressed as

$$Y = \begin{cases} x, & 0 < x < 4 \\ 4, & 4 \le x \end{cases}$$

We need to find $V(Y) = E(Y^2) - E(Y)^2$.

$$E(Y) = \int_0^4 x\left(\tfrac{1}{5}\right) dx + \int_4^5 4\left(\tfrac{1}{5}\right) dx = \tfrac{x^2}{10}\Big|_0^4 + \tfrac{4}{5} = 2.4$$

$$E(Y^2) = \int_0^4 x^2\left(\tfrac{1}{5}\right) dx + \int_4^5 4^2\left(\tfrac{1}{5}\right) dx = \tfrac{x^3}{15}\Big|_0^4 + \tfrac{16}{5} = 7.46\overline{6}$$

$$V(Y) = E(Y^2) - E(Y)^2 = 7.46\overline{6} - 2.4^2 = 1.7067$$

9-33.   Let X denote the random variable of repair cost and Y the random variable for the amount paid by the insurance. We need to find the standard deviation $\sigma_Y = \sqrt{V(Y)}$. Y can be written as

$$Y = \begin{cases} 0, & 0 < x \le 250 \\ x - 250, & 250 < x \end{cases}$$

The density function of X is $f(x) = \tfrac{1}{1500}$ on the interval $(0, 1500)$ We will use this to find $V(Y) = E(Y^2) - E(Y)^2$.

$$E(Y) = \int_0^{250} 0\left(\tfrac{1}{1500}\right) dx + \int_{250}^{1500} (x - 250)\left(\tfrac{1}{1500}\right) dx$$

$$= \frac{(x-250)^2}{3000}\Big|_{250}^{1500} = 520.833$$

$$E(Y^2) = \int_0^{250} 0\left(\tfrac{1}{1500}\right) dx + \int_{250}^{1500} (x - 250)^2 \left(\tfrac{1}{1500}\right) dx$$

$$= \frac{(x-250)^3}{4500}\Big|_{250}^{1500} = 434,027.778$$

$$V(Y) = E(Y^2) - E(Y)^2 = 434,027.778 - 520.833^2$$

$$= 162,760.76$$

$$\sigma_Y = \sqrt{V(Y)} = \sqrt{162,760.76} = 403.436$$

9-34. Let X denote the random variable for a loss. The cumulate density function for X is

$$F(x) = 1 - e^{-x/300}, \text{ for } x \geq 0.$$

To find the 95th percentile of actual losses that exceed the deductible, we need the cumulative distribution function for claims that are greater than 100, i.e., $F(x | X > 100)$.

$$
\begin{aligned}
F(x | X > 100) &= P(X \leq x | X > 100) \\
&= \frac{P(X \leq x \ \& \ X > 100)}{P(X > 100)} \\
&= \frac{P(100 < X \leq x)}{P(X > 100)} = \frac{F(x) - F(100)}{1 - F(100)} = \frac{e^{-1/3} - e^{-x/300}}{e^{-1/3}}
\end{aligned}
$$

To find the 95th percentile, we set

$$\frac{e^{-1/3} - e^{-x/300}}{e^{-1/3}} = .95$$

$$e^{-x/300} = .03583 - \frac{x}{300} = \ln(.03583) = -3.32907$$

$$x = 998.72$$

9-35. We will first find the cumulative distribution function for Y.

$$
\begin{aligned}
F_Y(y) = P(Y \leq y) &= P(T^2 \leq y) \\
&= P\left(T \leq \sqrt{y}\right) = F_T\left(\sqrt{y}\right) \\
&= 1 - \left(\frac{2}{\sqrt{y}}\right)^2 = 1 - \frac{4}{y}
\end{aligned}
$$

Then the density function for Y is

$$f_Y(y) = \frac{d}{dy} F_Y(y) = \frac{d}{dy}\left(1 - \frac{4}{y}\right) = \frac{4}{y^2}.$$

9-36. R is uniform on $(0.04, 0.08)$ and thus has cumulative distribution
function

$$F_R(r) = \frac{r - .04}{.04}, \quad \text{for} \quad 0.04 \le r \le 0.08$$

We need to find the cumulative distribution function for V.

$$F(v) = P(V \le v) = P(10{,}000 e^R \le v)$$
$$= P\left(R \le \ln\left(\frac{v}{10{,}000}\right)\right)$$
$$= F_R\left(\ln\left(\frac{v}{10{,}000}\right)\right) = \frac{\ln\left(\frac{v}{10{,}000}\right) - .04}{.04}$$
$$= 25\left[\ln\left(\frac{v}{10{,}000}\right) - .04\right].$$

*Note: This problem assumes that you know or can easily derive
the cumulative distribution function for a uniform random
variable on the interval [a,b].*

$$F(x) = \frac{x - a}{b - a}$$

9-37.   We will first find the cumulative distribution function for Y. We
will make use of the fact that $F_X(x) = 1 - e^{-x}$.

$$F_Y(y) = P(Y \le y) = P(10 X^{.8} \le y)$$
$$= P\left(X^{.8} \le \frac{y}{10}\right) = P\left(X \le \left(\frac{y}{10}\right)^{1/.8}\right)$$
$$= F_X\left[\left(\frac{y}{10}\right)^{1.25}\right] = 1 - e^{-(y/10)^{1.25}}$$

Now we can differentiate to find the density function.

$$f_Y(y) = \frac{d}{dy} F_Y(y) = \frac{d}{dy}(1 - e^{-(.10y)^{1.25}})$$
$$= -e^{-(.10y)^{1.25}}\left[-1.25(.1y)^{.25}(.1)\right]$$
$$= .125 e^{-(.10y)^{1.25}}(.1y)^{.25}$$

9-38. This is a problem involving a function of a random variable, since the rate R in customers per minute is

$$R = \frac{\text{Number of calls}}{\text{Time for calls}} = \frac{10}{T}.$$

The cumulative distribution function for T is

$$F_T(t) = \frac{t-8}{4}, \text{ for } 8 \le t \le 12$$

The cumulative distribution function for R is

$$F_R(r) = P(R \le r) = P\left(\frac{10}{T} \le r\right)$$
$$= P\left(\frac{10}{r} \le T\right) = 1 - F_R\left(\frac{10}{r}\right)$$
$$= 1 - \left(\frac{\frac{10}{r}-8}{4}\right) = 3 - \frac{2.5}{r}.$$

Now we can differentiate to find the density function.

$$f_R(r) = \frac{d}{dr} F_R(r) = \frac{d}{dr}\left(3 - \frac{2.5}{r}\right) = \frac{2.5}{r^2} = \frac{5}{2r^2}$$

9-39. Let X be the profit random variable for Company I and Y be the profit random variable for Company II. We are given that $Y = 2X$.

The cumulative distribution function for Y is

$$F_Y(y) = P(Y \le y) = P(2X \le y)$$
$$= P\left(X \le \frac{y}{2}\right) = F_X\left(\frac{y}{2}\right).$$

Now we can differentiate to find the density function.

$$f_Y(y) = \frac{d}{dy} F_Y(y) = \frac{d}{dy} F_X\left(\frac{y}{2}\right) = f_X\left(\frac{y}{2}\right)\left[\frac{1}{2}\right]$$

9-40. This one is tricky, since the distribution is mixed even though that is not explicitly stated. Note that

$$F(1) = \frac{1^2 - 2(1) + 2}{2} = \frac{1}{2}.$$

Since $F(x) = 0$ for $x < 0$, there is a discrete probability of $\frac{1}{2}$ at $x = 1$. The density function is

$$f(x) = \begin{cases} 0, & \text{for } x < 1 \\ \frac{1}{2}, & \text{for } x = 1 \\ x - 1 & \text{for } 1 < x \le 2 \\ 0 & \text{for } x > 2 \end{cases}$$

This requires a mixed calculation for $E(X)$ and $E(X^2)$.

$$E(X) = 1\left(\frac{1}{2}\right) + \int_1^2 x(x-1)\,dx = \frac{4}{3}$$

$$E(X^2) = 1^2\left(\frac{1}{2}\right) + \int_1^2 x^2(x-1)\,dx = \frac{23}{12}$$

$$V(X) = E(X^2) - E(X)^2 = \frac{23}{12} - \left(\frac{4}{3}\right)^2 = \frac{5}{36}$$

CHAPTER 10

10-1. The values of $p(x,y)$ can be found by direct substitution, e.g.
$$p(1,1) = P(X=1, Y=1) = \frac{(1)(1)+1}{27} = \frac{2}{27}.$$

The marginal probabilities can be found by adding the entries in the columns to get $p(x)$ and the row entries to get $p(y)$.

$$P(X=1) = p(1,1) + p(1,2) = \frac{2}{27} + \frac{4}{27} = \frac{2}{9}$$
$$P(Y=1) = p(1,1) + p(2,1) + p(3,1) = \frac{2}{27} + \frac{3}{27} + \frac{4}{27} = \frac{1}{3}$$

10-2. Since the team consists of 2 professionals the possible values of X and Y are $0 \le X+Y \le 2$, (2 CPA's and 1 actuary would be impossible). The event $(X=x, Y=y)$, denotes a team of x CPA's, y actuaries, and $2-(x+y)$ accountants.

$$P(X=0,Y=0) = p(0,0) = \frac{C(5,0)C(3,0)C(2,2)}{C(10,2)} = \frac{1}{45}$$
$$P(X=0,Y=1) = p(0,1) = \frac{C(5,0)C(3,1)C(2,1)}{45} = \frac{6}{45}$$
$$P(X=1,Y=0) = p(1,0) = \frac{C(5,1)C(3,0)C(2,1)}{45} = \frac{10}{45}$$
$$P(X=1,Y=1) = p(1,1) = \frac{C(5,1)C(3,1)C(2,0)}{45} = \frac{15}{45}, \text{ etc.}$$

The marginal probabilities can be found by obtaining row sums and column sums as in 10-1.

$$P(X=0) = p(0,0) + p(0,1) + p(0,2) = \frac{1}{45} + \frac{6}{45} + \frac{3}{45} = \frac{10}{45}$$

10-3.   Using the table obtained in Exercise 10-1:

$$E(X) = \sum x p_X(x) = \tfrac{2}{9} + 2\left(\tfrac{3}{9}\right) + 3\left(\tfrac{4}{9}\right) = \tfrac{20}{9}$$

$$E(Y) = \sum y p_Y(y) = \tfrac{1}{3} + 2\left(\tfrac{2}{3}\right) = \tfrac{5}{3}$$

10-4.   Using the table obtained in Exercise 10-2:

$$E(X) = \sum x p_X(x) = 0 + \tfrac{25}{45} + 2\left(\tfrac{10}{45}\right) = 1$$

$$E(Y) = \sum y p_Y(y) = 0 + \tfrac{21}{45} + 2\left(\tfrac{3}{45}\right) = \tfrac{27}{45} = \tfrac{3}{5}$$

10-5.   Using the table from Exercise 10-2:

$$E(X^2) = \sum x^2 p_X(x) = 0 + 1^2\left(\tfrac{25}{45}\right) + 2^2\left(\tfrac{10}{45}\right) = \tfrac{65}{45} = \tfrac{13}{9}$$

$$V(X) = E(X^2) - E(X)^2 = \tfrac{13}{9} - 1 = \tfrac{4}{9}$$

$$E(Y^2) = \sum y^2 p_Y(y) = 0 + 1^2\left(\tfrac{21}{45}\right) + 2^2\left(\tfrac{3}{45}\right) = \tfrac{33}{45} = \tfrac{11}{15}$$

$$V(Y) = \tfrac{11}{15} - \left(\tfrac{3}{5}\right)^2 = \tfrac{55-27}{75} = \tfrac{28}{75}$$

10-6.   Clearly the function $f(x,y) = \tfrac{1}{4} + \tfrac{x}{2} + \tfrac{y}{2} + xy,\ 0 \le x \le 1$ and $0 \le y \le 1$, is greater than or equal to 0 on this range, so we only need to show that the volume under the surface is 1.

$$\int_0^1 \int_0^1 \left(\tfrac{1}{4} + \tfrac{x}{2} + \tfrac{y}{2} + xy\right) dx\, dy = \int_0^1 \left(\tfrac{x}{4} + \tfrac{x^2}{4} + \tfrac{xy}{2} + \tfrac{x^2 y}{2}\right)\Big|_{x=0}^{1} dy$$

$$= \int_0^1 \left(\tfrac{1}{2} + y\right) dy$$

$$= \left(\tfrac{y}{2} + \tfrac{y^2}{2}\Big|_0^1\right) = 1$$

Therefore f(x,y) is a joint probability density function.

$$P\left(0 \le X \le \tfrac{1}{2}, \tfrac{1}{2} \le Y \le 1\right) = \int_{1/2}^{1} \int_{0}^{1/2} \left(\tfrac{1}{4} + \tfrac{x}{2} + \tfrac{y}{x} + xy\right) dx\, dy$$

$$= \int_{1/2}^{1} \left(\tfrac{x}{4} + \tfrac{x^2}{4} + \tfrac{xy}{2} + \tfrac{x^2 y}{2}\right)\Bigg|_{x=0}^{1/2} dy$$

$$= \int_{1/2}^{1} \left(\tfrac{3}{16} + \tfrac{3y}{8}\right) dy$$

$$= \left(\tfrac{3y}{16} + \tfrac{3y^2}{16}\right)\Bigg|_{1/2}^{1} = \tfrac{15}{64}$$

10-7. (a) $f_X(x) = \int_{0}^{1} f(x,y)\, dy$

$$= \int_{0}^{1} \left(\tfrac{1}{4} + \tfrac{x}{2} + \tfrac{y}{2} + xy\right) dy$$

$$= \left(\tfrac{y}{4} + \tfrac{xy}{4} + \tfrac{y^2}{4} + \tfrac{xy^2}{2}\right)\Bigg|_{y=0}^{1} = \left(\tfrac{1}{2} + x\right), \quad 0 \le x \le 1$$

(b) $f_Y(y) = \int_{0}^{1} f(x,y)\, dx$

$$= \int_{0}^{1} \left(\tfrac{1}{4} + \tfrac{x}{2} + \tfrac{y}{2} + xy\right) dx$$

$$= \left(\tfrac{x}{4} + \tfrac{x^2}{4} + \tfrac{xy}{4} + \tfrac{x^2 y}{2}\right)\Bigg|_{x=0}^{1} = \left(\tfrac{1}{2} + y\right), \quad 0 \le y \le 1$$

10-8. The density function $f(x,y) = 2x^2 + 3y$ is defined on the region bounded by the x-axis and the lines $y = x$ and $x = 1$.

(a) $f_X(x) = \int_{0}^{x} (2x^2 + 3y)\, dy = \left(2x^2 y + \tfrac{3y^2}{2}\right)\Bigg|_{y=0}^{x}$

$$= 2x^3 + \tfrac{3x^2}{2}, \quad 0 \le x \le 1$$

(b) $f_Y(y) = \int_{y}^{1} (2x^2 + 3y)\, dx = \left(\tfrac{2x^3}{3} + 3xy\right)\Bigg|_{x=y}^{1}$

$$= \tfrac{2}{3} + 3y - 3y^2 - \left(\tfrac{2}{3}\right)y^3, \quad 0 \le y \le 1$$

10-9. Using the marginal distributions from Exercise 10-8:

(a) $P\left(X > \frac{1}{2}\right) = \int_{1/2}^{1}\left(2x^3 + \frac{3x^2}{2}\right) dx$

$= \left(\frac{x^4}{2} + \frac{x^3}{2}\right)\Big|_{1/2}^{1} = \frac{29}{32}$

(b) $P\left(Y > \frac{1}{2}\right) = \int_{1/2}^{1}\left(\frac{2}{3} + 3y - 3y^2 - \frac{2y^3}{3}\right) dy$

$= \left(\frac{2y}{3} + \frac{3y^2}{2} - y^3 - \frac{y^4}{6}\right)\Big|_{1/2}^{1} = \frac{41}{96}$

10-10. From Exercise 10-6, $f_X(x) = \frac{1}{2} + x$ for $0 \le x \le 1$.

$E(X) = \int_0^1 x\left(\frac{1}{2} + x\right) dx = \int_0^1\left(\frac{x}{2} + x^2\right) dx$

$= \left(\frac{x^2}{4} + \frac{x^3}{3}\right)\Big|_0^1 = \frac{7}{12}$

10-11. If $f(x,y) = \frac{1}{4} + \frac{x}{2} + \frac{y}{2} + xy$, for $0 \le x \le 1$ and $0 \le y \le 1$, then

$P(X > Y) = \int_0^1 \int_0^x \left(\frac{1}{4} + \frac{x}{2} + \frac{y}{2} + xy\right) dy\, dx$

$= \int_0^1 \left(\frac{y}{4} + \frac{xy}{2} + \frac{y^2}{4} + \frac{xy^2}{2}\right)\Big|_{y=0}^{x} dx$

$= \int_0^1 \left(\frac{x}{4} + \frac{3x^2}{4} + \frac{x^3}{2}\right) dx$

$= \left(\frac{x^2}{8} + \frac{x^3}{4} + \frac{x^4}{8}\right)\Big|_0^1 = \frac{1}{2}$

10-12. From Exercise 10-8, $f_X(x) = 2x^3 + \frac{3x^2}{2}$, for $0 \le x \le 1$.

$$E(X) = \int_0^1 x f_X(x)dx = \int_0^1 \left(2x^4 + \frac{3x^3}{2}\right)dx$$

$$= \left(\frac{2x^5}{5} + \frac{3x^4}{8}\right)\Big|_0^1 = \frac{31}{40}$$

Also $f_y(y) = \frac{2}{3} + 3y - 3y^2 - \frac{2y^3}{3}$, for $0 \le y \le 1$.

$$E(Y) = \int_0^1 y f_Y(y)dy = \int_0^1 \left(\frac{2y}{3} + 3y^2 - 3y^3 + \frac{2y^4}{3}\right)dy$$

$$= \left(\frac{y^2}{3} + y^3 - \frac{3y^4}{4} - \frac{2y^5}{15}\right)\Big|_0^1 = \frac{9}{20}$$

10-13. $f(x,y) = \frac{30-x-y}{1875}$, for $0 \le x \le 5$ and $0 \le y \le 25$.

$$P(X \ge 4, Y \ge 20) = \frac{1}{1875} \int_{20}^{25} \int_4^5 (30-x-y)\,dxdy$$

$$= \frac{1}{1875} \int_{20}^{25} \left(30x - \frac{x^2}{2} - xy\right)\Big|_{x=4}^5 dy$$

$$= \frac{1}{3750} \int_{20}^{25} (51 - 2y)dy$$

$$= \left(\frac{1}{3750}\right)(51y - y^2)\Big|_{20}^{25} = \frac{30}{3750} = \frac{1}{125}$$

10-14. (a) $f_X(x) = \int_0^{25} \left(\frac{30-x-y}{1875}\right)dy = \left(\frac{30y - xy - y^2/2}{1875}\right)\Big|_{y=0}^{25}$

$$= \left(\frac{60y - 2xy - y^2}{3750}\right)_{y=0}^{25}$$

$$= \frac{875 - 50x}{3750}$$

$$= \frac{35 - 2x}{150}, \quad \text{for } 0 \le x \le 5$$

(b) $f_Y(y) = \int_0^5 \left(\frac{30-x-y}{1875}\right) dx$

$= \left(\frac{30x - x^2/2 - xy}{1875}\right)_{x=0}^5$

$= \left(\frac{60 - x^2 - 2xy}{3750}\right)_{x=0}^5$

$= \frac{275 - 10y}{3750} = \frac{55 - 2y}{750}, \quad for \ \ 0 \le y \le 25$

10-15. For the random variables in Exercise 10-13:

$E(X) = \int_0^5 x f_X(x) dx = \left(\frac{1}{150}\right) \int_0^5 (35x - 2x^2) \, dx$

$= \left(\frac{1}{150}\right)\left(\frac{35x^2}{2} - \frac{2x^3}{3}\right)_0^5 = \frac{2125}{900} = \frac{85}{36}$

$E(Y) = \int_0^{25} y f_Y(y) \, dy = \left(\frac{1}{750}\right) \int_0^{25} (55y - 2y^2) \, dy$

$= \left(\frac{1}{750}\right)\left(\frac{55y^2}{2} - \frac{2y^3}{3}\right)_0^{25}$

$= \frac{40,625}{6 \cdot 750} = \frac{325}{36}$

10-16. Using the data from the table obtained in Exercise 10-1:

$P(X=1 \mid Y=1) = \frac{p(1,1)}{p_Y(1)} = \frac{2/27}{1/3} = \frac{2}{9}$

$P(X=2 \mid Y=1) = \frac{p(2,1)}{p_Y(1)} = \frac{1/9}{1/3} = \frac{1}{3}$

$P(X=3 \mid Y=1) = \frac{p(3,1)}{p_Y(1)} = \frac{4/27}{1/3} = \frac{4}{9}$

10-17. Using the data from the table obtained in Exercise 10-1:

$P(Y=1 \mid X=1) = \frac{p(1,1)}{p_X(1)} = \frac{2/27}{2/9} = \frac{1}{3}$

$P(Y=2 \mid X=1) = \frac{p(1,2)}{p_X(1)} = \frac{4/27}{2/9} = \frac{2}{3}$

10-18. Using the data obtained in Exercise 10-16:

$$E(X\,|\,Y=1) \;=\; \sum xP(X=x\,|\,Y=1)$$
$$= 1\left(\tfrac{2}{9}\right)+2\left(\tfrac{1}{3}\right)+3\left(\tfrac{4}{9}\right) \;=\; \tfrac{20}{9}$$

10-19. For the joint density function in Exercise 10-6:

$$f(x\,|\,y) \;=\; \frac{f(x,y)}{f_Y(y)} \;=\; \frac{1/4+x/2+y/2+xy}{1/2+y}$$
$$= \frac{(1/2+x)(1/2+y)}{(1/2+y)} \;=\; \tfrac{1}{2}+x, \quad 0\le x\le 1$$

10-20. For the joint density function in Exercise 10-8:

$$f(y\,|\,x) \;=\; \frac{f(x,y)}{f_X(x)} \;=\; \frac{2x^2+3y}{2x^3+3x^2/2}, \quad \text{for } 0<y\le x\le 1$$

10-21. (a) $f\left(y\,|\,\tfrac{1}{2}\right) = \dfrac{2(1/2)^2+3y}{2(1/2)^3+(3/2)(1/2)^2} = \dfrac{4+24y}{5}, \quad 0<y\le\tfrac{1}{2}$

(b) $E\left(Y\,|\,X=\tfrac{1}{2}\right) = \displaystyle\int_0^{1/2} y f\left(y\,|\,\tfrac{1}{2}\right) dy$

$$= \left(\tfrac{1}{5}\right)\int_0^{1/2}(4y+24y^2)\,dy$$
$$= \left(\tfrac{1}{5}\right)(2y^2+8y^3)\Big|_0^{1/2} \;=\; \tfrac{3}{10}$$

10-22. Let $f(x,y)=6x$, for $0<x<y<1$, and 0 elsewhere.

(a) $f_Y(y) = \displaystyle\int_0^y f(x,y)\,dx = \int_0^y 6x\,dx = 3y^2$, for $0<y<1$

(b) $f(x\,|\,y) = \dfrac{f(x,y)}{f_Y(y)} = \dfrac{6x}{3y^2} = \dfrac{2x}{y^2}$, for $0<x<y<1$

(c) $E(X\,|\,Y=y) = \displaystyle\int_0^y x f(x\,|\,y)\,dx = \left(\tfrac{1}{y^2}\right)\int_0^y 2x^2\,dx = \tfrac{1}{y^2}\cdot\tfrac{2y^3}{3} = \tfrac{2y}{3}$

(d) $E\left(X\,|\,Y=\tfrac{1}{2}\right) = \dfrac{2\cdot 1/2}{3} = \tfrac{1}{3}$

10-23. Let X and Y be the random variables in Exercise 10-1. From the
        table obtained in that exercise it can be seen that

$$p(x,y) = p_X(x)p_Y(y)$$

for all possible choices of x and y, e.g.,

$$p(1,1) = \tfrac{2}{27} = \left(\tfrac{2}{9}\right)\left(\tfrac{1}{3}\right) = p_X(1)p_Y(1)$$

$$p(2,1) = \tfrac{1}{9} = \left(\tfrac{1}{3}\right)\left(\tfrac{1}{3}\right) = p_X(2)p_Y(1), \text{ etc.}$$

Hence X and Y are independent.

10-24. Using the tables obtained for the random variables in Exercise
        10-2,
$$p(0,0) = \tfrac{1}{45} \neq \left(\tfrac{10}{45}\right)\left(\tfrac{21}{45}\right) = p_X(0)p_Y(0).$$

Hence X and Y are dependent.

10-25. In Exercise 10-6 the joint density function is

$$f(x,y) = \tfrac{1}{4} + \tfrac{x}{2} + \tfrac{y}{2} + xy = \left(\tfrac{1}{2}+x\right)\left(\tfrac{1}{2}+y\right) = f_X(x)f_Y(y).$$

Hence X and Y are independent.

10-26. For the joint density function $f(x,y)$ in Exercise 10-8,

$$f(x,y) = 2x^2 + 3y \neq \left(2x^3 + \tfrac{3x^2}{2}\right)\left(\tfrac{2}{3}+3y-3y^2-\tfrac{2y^3}{3}\right)$$
$$= f_X(x)f_Y(y).$$

Hence X and Y are dependent.

10-27. The doctor is looking at the bivariate distribution of blood pressure and heartbeat. The information given provides us with partial information for the bivariate probability table. We start with the marginal probabilities that are given.

Heartbeat Blood Pressure	Irregular I	Regular R	Marginal for Blood Pressure
High H			.14
Normal N			
Low L			.22
Marginal for Heartbeat	.15		1.00

Since marginal probabilities must total one, we can fill in the table in the margins. Those numbers are shaded in the margins below. Then we can use iv) and v) to fill in the joint probabilities for $P(H \& I) = \frac{1}{3}(.15) = .05$

$$P(N \& I) = \frac{1}{8}(.64) = .08.$$

Those numbers are italicized in the table.

Heartbeat Blood Pressure	Irregular I	Regular R	Marginal for Blood Pressure
High H	.05		.14
Normal N	.08		.64
Low L			.22
Marginal for Heartbeat	.15	.85	1.00

Finally, since each row or column of bivariate probabilities must add up to the marginal, we can complete the table.

Heartbeat Blood Pressure	Irregular I	Regular R	Marginal for Blood Pressure
High H	.05	.09	.14
Normal N	.08	.56	.64
Low L	.02	.20	.22
Marginal for Heartbeat	.15	.85	1.00

The probability of low blood pressure and a regular heartbeat is .20.

10-28. Let L, M and H denote the number of low risk, moderate risk and high risk drivers respectively. Then

$$p_1 = P(L) = .50, \quad p_2 = P(M) = .30 \quad p_3 = P(H) = .20.$$

There are only four ways that 4 will contain at least two more high-risk drivers than low-risk drivers. We show each and its multinomial probability below.

1) $L = 0$, $M = 0$ and $H = 4$. Then

$$P(L=0 \,\&\, M=0 \,\&\, H=4) = \binom{4}{0,0,4}.5^0.3^0.2^4$$
$$= 1(.5^0.3^0.2^4) = .0016$$

2) $L = 0$, $M = 1$ and $H = 3$. Then

$$P(L=0 \,\&\, M=1 \,\&\, H=3) = \binom{4}{0,1,3}.5^0.3^1.2^3$$
$$= 4(.5^0.3^1.2^3) = .0096$$

3) $L = 1$, $M = 0$ and $H = 3$. Then

$$P\left(L=1 \,\&\, M=0 \,\&\, H=3\right) = \binom{4}{1,0,3}.5^1.3^0.2^3$$
$$= 4(.5^1.3^0.2^3) = .0160$$

4) $L = 0$, $M = 2$ and $H = 2$. Then

$$P(L=0 \,\&\, M=2 \,\&\, H=2) = \binom{4}{0,2,2}.5^0.3^2.2^2$$
$$= 6(.5^0.3^2.2^2) = .0216$$

The sum of these probabilities is .0488.

10-29. The device fails if either $X < 1$ or $Y < 1$. The set of pairs (x, y) for which this occurs is shown in the lined region in the diagram below.

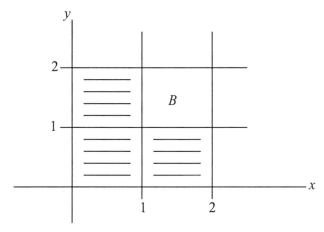

If we call this region A, $P(X < 1 \text{ or } Y < 1) = \iint_A f(x, y)\, dxdy$.

However we would need to integrate in two pieces to do this integral. Note that we can integrate over the unshaded rectangle B, to get the complementary probability, so that

$$P(X < 1 \text{ or } Y < 1) = 1 - \iint_B f(x, y)\, dxdy$$

$$= 1 - \int_1^2 \int_1^2 \left(\frac{x+y}{8}\right) dxdy$$

Thus we calculate

$$\int_1^2 \int_1^2 \left(\frac{x+y}{8}\right) dxdy = \frac{1}{8} \int_1^2 \left(\frac{x^2}{2} + xy\right)\Big|_1^2 dy$$

$$= \frac{1}{8} \int_1^2 (1.5 + y) dy = \frac{1}{8}\left(.5y + \frac{y^2}{2}\right)\Big|_1^2$$

$$= \frac{3}{8} = .375$$

$$P(X < 1 \text{ or } Y < 1) = 1 - .375 = .625$$

10-30. The device fails if either $X < 1$ or $Y < 1$. The set of pairs (x, y) for which this occurs is shown in the lined region in the diagram below.

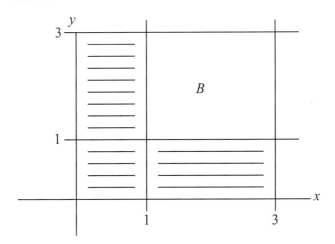

If we call this region A, $P(X < 1 \text{ or } Y < 1) = \iint_A f(x, y)\, dxdy$. We can integrate over the unshaded rectangle B, to get the complementary probability, so that

$$P(X < 1 \text{ or } Y < 1) = 1 - \iint_B f(x, y)\, dxdy$$

$$= 1 - \int_1^3 \int_1^3 \left(\frac{x + y}{27}\right) dxdy$$

Thus we calculate

$$\int_1^3 \int_1^3 \left(\frac{x+y}{27}\right) dxdy = \frac{1}{27} \int_1^3 \left(\frac{x^2}{2} + xy\right)\Big|_1^3 dy$$

$$= \frac{1}{27} \int_1^3 (4 + 2y)dy$$

$$= \frac{1}{27}\left(4y + y^2\right)\Big|_1^3 = \frac{16}{27} = .59$$

$$P(X < 1 \text{ or } Y < 1) = 1 - .59 = .41$$

10-31. The device fails if either $S < 1/2$ or $T < 1/2$. The set of pairs (x, y) for which this occurs is shown in the lined region in the diagram below.

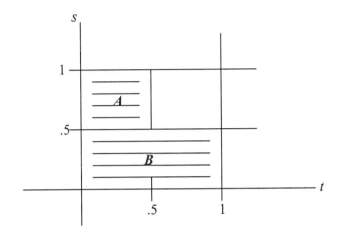

We have broken up the shaded region into two separate regions A and B.

$$P\left(S < \tfrac{1}{2} \text{ or } Y < \tfrac{1}{2}\right) = \iint_A f(s,t)\,dsdt + \iint_B f(s,t)\,dsdt$$
$$= \int_0^{0.5} \int_{0.5}^{1} f(s,t)\,dsdt + \int_0^{1} \int_0^{0.5} f(s,t)\,dsdt \ .$$

10-32. We need $P(X \geq 20 \,\&\, Y \geq 20)$. The density function is non-zero only in the first quadrant triangle bounded above by the line $x + y = 50$ or $y = 50 - x$. In the next diagram we show the triangle and the region R where $X \geq 20 \,\&\, Y \geq 20$.

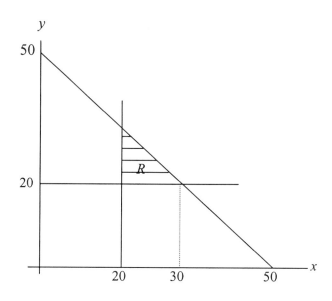

$$P(X \geq 20 \,\&\, Y \geq 20) = \iint_R f(x,y)\, dydx$$

$$= \frac{6}{125,000} \int_{20}^{30} \int_{20}^{50-x} (50-x-y)\, dydx$$

10-33. Let X be the time until the next Basic Policy claim and Y the time until the next Deluxe policy claim. We need to find $P(X > Y)$.

Since X has mean $E(X) = \frac{1}{\lambda} = 2$, the density function for X has $\lambda = \frac{1}{2}$. Similarly, the density function for Y has $\lambda = \frac{1}{3}$. Then the density functions for X and Y are

$$f_X(x) = \tfrac{1}{2}e^{-x/2} \text{ and } f_Y(y) = \tfrac{1}{3}e^{-y/3}.$$

Since X and Y are independent, the joint density function is

$$f(x,y) = f_X(x)f_Y(y) = \tfrac{1}{6}e^{-x/2}e^{-y/3} \text{ for } x \geq 0 \text{ and } y \geq 0$$

The region in which $X > Y$ is the region in the first quadrant below the line $y = x$.

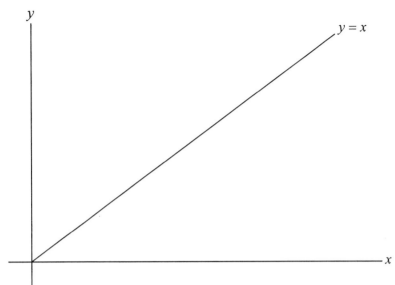

The integral calculation is shown below

$$P(X > Y) = \int_0^\infty \int_0^x f(x,y)\, dy dx$$

$$= \int_0^\infty \int_0^x \frac{1}{6} e^{-x/2} e^{-y/3}\, dy dx$$

$$= \frac{1}{6} \int_0^\infty e^{-x/2} \int_0^x e^{-y/3}\, dy dx$$

$$= \frac{1}{6} \int_0^\infty e^{-x/2} \left(-3 e^{-y/3}\right)\Big|_0^x\, dx$$

$$= \frac{1}{6} \int_0^\infty e^{-x/2} 3(1 - e^{-x/3})\, dx$$

$$= \frac{1}{2} \int_0^\infty (e^{-x/2} - e^{-5x/6})\, dx$$

$$= \frac{1}{2} \left(-2 e^{-x/2} + \frac{6}{5} e^{-5/6}\right)\Big|_0^\infty$$

$$= \frac{1}{2}\left(2 - \frac{6}{5}\right) = \frac{1}{2}\left(\frac{4}{5}\right) = \frac{2}{5}$$

10-34. Let X and Y be the random variables for the bids from the two companies. The two bids are considered further if they differ by less than 20. Thus we need to find

$$P(|X-Y| < 20) = P(-20 < X-Y < 20).$$

Note that X and Y are independent, each with density function $f(x) = \frac{1}{200}$ for $2000 < x < 2200.$ Thus the joint distribution function is

$$f(x,y) = \left(\frac{1}{200}\right)^2 = \frac{1}{40,000}$$

for $2000 \le x \le 2200$ and $2000 \le y \le 2200$

The points (x,y) for which $-20 < X-Y < 20$ are in the region R pictured below bounded by the two straight lines $y = x+20$ and $y = x-20.$

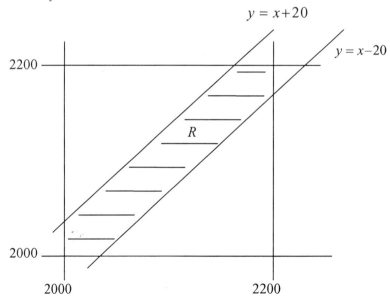

Since $f(x,y) = \frac{1}{40,000}$ is constant we can avoid integrating.

$$P(-20 < X - Y < 20) = \iint_R f(x,y)\,dy\,dx = \left(\frac{1}{40,000}\right)(\text{area of } R)$$

The area of R can be written as the area of the square less the areas of the two unshaded triangles, i.e.,

$$40,000 - 2\left(\frac{180^2}{2}\right) = 7600.$$

Thus $P(-20 < X - Y < 20) = \frac{7,600}{40,000} = .19.$

10-35   We first put the given information into a bivariate table, since this makes it easy to fill in the marginal probabilities for X. Note that the given probabilities add up to one, so that the probability of any other (x, y) pair is 0.

Y \ X	0	1	2
0	$\frac{1}{6}$	$\frac{1}{12}$	$\frac{1}{12}$
1	0	$\frac{1}{6}$	$\frac{1}{3}$
2	0	0	$\frac{1}{6}$
$p_X(x)$	$\frac{1}{6} = \frac{2}{12}$	$\frac{3}{12}$	$\frac{7}{12}$

Now the variance of X can be calculated directly.

$$E(X) = 0\left(\frac{2}{12}\right) + 1\left(\frac{3}{12}\right) + 2\left(\frac{7}{12}\right) = \frac{17}{12}$$

$$E(X^2) = 0^2\left(\frac{2}{12}\right) + 1^2\left(\frac{3}{12}\right) + 2^2\left(\frac{7}{12}\right) = \frac{31}{12}$$

$$V(X) = \frac{31}{12} - \left(\frac{17}{12}\right)^2 = .576$$

10-36. We need to find the conditional density function $f\left(y \mid X = \tfrac{1}{3}\right)$,

since $P\left(Y < X \mid X = \tfrac{1}{3}\right)$ will be obtained by integrating that density. It is a good idea to start with a diagram to help with the limits of integration. The density $f(x,y)$ is non zero on the first quadrant triangle bounded above by the line $y = 1-x$ or $x+y = 1$.

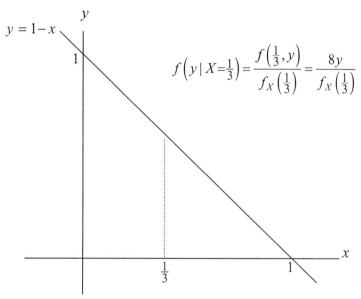

$$f\left(y \mid X = \tfrac{1}{3}\right) = \frac{f\left(\tfrac{1}{3}, y\right)}{f_X\left(\tfrac{1}{3}\right)} = \frac{8y}{f_X\left(\tfrac{1}{3}\right)}$$

We need to calculate $f_X\left(\tfrac{1}{3}\right)$

$$f_X(x) = \int_0^{1-x} (24xy)\,dy = 12xy^2 \Big|_0^{1-x} = 12x(1-x)^2 \rightarrow$$

$$f_X\left(\tfrac{1}{3}\right) = 12\left(\tfrac{1}{3}\right)\left(\tfrac{2}{3}\right)^2 = \left(\tfrac{16}{9}\right).$$

Thus

$$f\left(y \mid X = \tfrac{1}{3}\right) = \frac{8y}{(16/9)} = \frac{9y}{2} = 4.5y$$

$$P\left(Y < X \mid X = \tfrac{1}{3}\right) = \int_0^{1/3} \left(f\left(y \mid X = \tfrac{1}{3}\right)\right) dy$$

$$= \int_0^{1/3} (4.5y)\,dy = 4.5\left(\frac{y^2}{2}\right)\Big|_0^{1/3} = .25 = \tfrac{1}{4}$$

10-37. The required answer is to find $P(1 < Y < 3 \mid X = 2)$. We need to find the conditional density function $f(y \mid X = 2)$ to evaluate that conditional probability.

$$f(y \mid X = 2) = \frac{f(2,y)}{f_X(2)} = \frac{.5y^{-3}}{f_X(2)}$$

Thus we need to find

$$f_X(2) = \int_1^\infty f(2,y)dy = \int_1^\infty .5y^{-3}dy = \left. \frac{-y^{-2}}{-4} \right|_1^\infty = \frac{1}{4}$$

Then

$$f(y \mid X = 2) = \frac{.5y^{-3}}{f_X(2)} = \frac{.5y^{-3}}{1/4} = 2y^{-3}$$

$$P(1 < Y < 3 \mid X = 2) = \int_1^3 f(y \mid X = 2)dy$$

$$= \int_1^3 2y^{-3}dy = \left. -y^{-2} \right|_1^3 = \frac{8}{9}$$

10-38. Note that both X and Y must be restricted to the interval $[0,1]$, since they both represent a percent of employees, and that $X \geq Y$, since the buyers of supplemental policies are a subset of the buyers of basic policies. Thus we can express the density function more explicitly as

$$f(x,y) = 2(x+y) \quad \text{for} \quad 0 \leq y \leq x \leq 1.$$

The required answer is to find $P(Y < .05 \mid X = .10)$. We need to find the conditional density function $f(y \mid X = .10)$ to evaluate that conditional probability

$$f(y \mid X = .10) = \frac{f(.10,y)}{f_X(.10)} = \frac{2(.10+y)}{f_X(.10)}$$

Thus we need to find

$$f_X(.1) = \int_0^{0.1} f(.1,y)\, dy = \int_0^{0.1} (.2+2y)\, dy$$

$$= .2y + y^2 \Big|_0^{0.1} = .03$$

Note that the upper limit on the integral above was .1, since it is required that we have $y \le x$.

Then

$$f(y\,|\,X=.10) = \frac{f(.10,y)}{f_X(.10)} = \frac{2(.10+y)}{.03} = \frac{20}{3} + \frac{200}{3}y$$

$$P(Y<.05\,|\,X=.10) = \int_0^{.05}\left(\frac{20}{3} + \frac{200}{3}y\right) dy$$

$$= \left(\frac{20y}{3} + \frac{200}{6}y^2\right)\Big|_0^{.05} = .4167$$

10-39. This is a conditional expectation problem. Let H be the event that the husband survives at least ten years and W be the event that the wife survives at least ten years. The premiums are already paid for $2(500)=1000$. Thus we need to find

$$1,000 - E(benefits\,|\,H).$$

If the husband survives 10 years, the only way a benefit can be paid during that 10 years is if the wife dies. To find the conditional expectation we need to find

$$P(W\,|\,H) = \frac{P(W\cap H)}{P(H)} \quad \text{and} \quad P(\sim W\,|\,H) = \frac{P(\sim W\cap H)}{P(H)}.$$

We will use a Venn diagram as an aid.

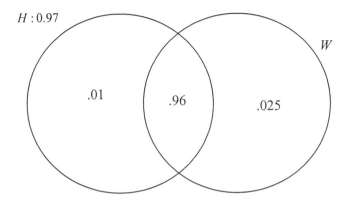

The statement that "the probability that only the husband will survive at least ten years is 0.01" tells us that $P(\sim W \cap H) = .01$. We are also given that $P(W \cap H) = .96$. As we can see from the Venn diagram, $P(H) = P(W \cap H) + P(\sim W \cap H) = .97$. Now we can fill out the conditional distribution for the wife given that the husband survives.

$$P(W \mid H) = \frac{P(W \cap H)}{P(H)} = \frac{96}{97}$$

and

$$P(\sim W \mid H) = \frac{P(\sim W \cap H)}{P(H)} = \frac{1}{97}$$

A benefit of 10,000 is paid if the wife dies, and no benefit is paid otherwise. The expected benefit if the wife dies given that the husband has survived is

$$10,000\left(\tfrac{1}{97}\right) + 0\left(\tfrac{96}{97}\right) = 103.09$$

Thus

$$1,000 - E(benefits \mid H) = 1000 - 103.09 = 896.91$$

10-40. We can calculate this variance if we know the conditional distribution of Y given that $X = 1$. First we will put the given probability values in a table that also shows the marginal probabilities for X.

X \ Y	0	1
0	.800	.050
1	.025	.125
$p_X(x)$	.825	.175

The conditional probabilities of Y given that $X = 1$ are

$$P(Y=0 \mid X=1) = \frac{P(Y=0 \& X=1)}{P(X=1)} = \frac{.05}{.175} = .2857$$

$$P(Y=1 \mid X=1) = \frac{P(Y=1 \& X=1)}{P(X=1)} = \frac{.125}{.175} = .7143$$

Then we can calculate the variance using the identity

$$V(X) = E(X^2) - E(X)^2$$

$$E(Y \mid X=1) = .2857(0) + .7143(1) = .7143$$

$$E(Y^2 \mid X=1) = .2857(0)^2 + .7143(1)^2 = .7143$$

$$V(X) = .7143 - (.7143)^2 = .204$$

10-41. We can calculate this variance if we know the conditional distribution of Y given that $X=x$.

$$f(y \mid X=x) = \frac{f(x,y)}{f_X(x)} = \frac{2x}{f_X(x)}$$

for $0 < x < 1$ and $x < y < x+1$

Note that when we integrate with respect to y the limits of integration will be x and x+1, due to the restrictions on y.

We need to find for $0 \le x \le 1$,

$$f_X(x) = \int_x^{x+1} f(x,y)\, dy = \int_x^{x+1} 2x\, dy$$
$$= 2xy\Big|_x^{x+1} = 2x(x+1) - 2x^2 = 2x$$

This give us $f(y\,|\,X=x) = 1$ for $0 < x < 1$ and $x < y < x+1$.
Then we can calculate the variance using the identity
$V(X) = E(X^2) - E(X)^2$.

$$E(Y\,|\,X=x) = \int_x^{x+1} y\, dy = \frac{y^2}{2}\Big|_x^{x+1} = \frac{(x+1)^2}{2} - \frac{x^2}{2} = x + \tfrac{1}{2}$$

$$E(Y^2\,|\,X=x) = \int_x^{x+1} y^2\, dy$$
$$= \frac{y^3}{3}\Big|_x^{x+1} = \frac{(x+1)^3}{3} - \frac{x^3}{3} = x^2 + x + \tfrac{1}{3}$$

$$V(Y\,|\,X=x) = x^2 + x + \tfrac{1}{3} - \left(x + \tfrac{1}{2}\right)^2 = \tfrac{1}{3} - \tfrac{1}{4} = \tfrac{1}{12}$$

10-42. Let P be the number of tornados in county P and Q be the number of tornados in county Q. We need to find $V(Q\,|\,P=0)$. We can calculate this variance if we know the conditional distribution of Q given that $P = 0$. For this we will need to know the marginal

$$\Pr[P=0] = p_P(0) = .12 + .06 + .05 + .02 = .25$$

The required conditional probabilities are

$$\Pr[Q=0\,|\,P=0] = \frac{\Pr[Q=0\&P=0]}{\Pr(P=0)} = \frac{.12}{.25} = .48$$

$$\Pr[Q=1\,|\,P=0] = \frac{\Pr[Q=1\&P=0]}{\Pr(P=0)} = \frac{.06}{.25} = .24$$

$$\Pr[Q=2\,|\,P=0] = \frac{\Pr[Q=2\&P=0]}{\Pr(P=0)} = \frac{.05}{.25} = .20$$

$$\Pr[Q=3\,|\,P=0] = \frac{\Pr[Q=3\&P=0]}{\Pr(P=0)} = \frac{.02}{.25} = .08$$

Then we can calculate the variance using the identity

$$V(X) = E(X^2) - E(X)^2$$
$$E(Q\,|\,P{=}0) = .48(0) + .24(1) + .20(2) + .08(3) = .88$$
$$E(Q\,|\,P{=}0) = .48(0)^2 + .24(1)^2 + .20(2)^2 + .08(3)^2 = 1.76$$
$$V(X) = 1.76 - (.88)^2 = .9856$$

10-43.   We need to find $P(X < .2) = \iint_A f(x,y)\,dydx$, where A is the region indicated in the diagram below.

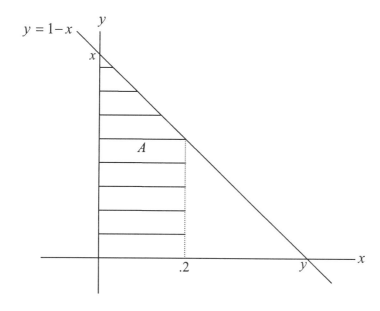

$$\iint_A f(x,y)\,dydx \;=\; 6\int_0^{.2}\int_0^{1-x}[1-x-y]\,dydx$$

$$=\; 6\int_0^{.2}\left(y-xy-\frac{y^2}{2}\right)\Bigg|_0^{1-x} dx$$

$$=\; 6\int_0^{.2}\left((1-x)-x(1-x)-\frac{(1-x)^2}{2}\right)dx$$

$$=\; 6\int_0^{.2}\frac{(1-x)^2}{2}dx \;=\; 6\left[\frac{-(1-x)^3}{6}\right]_0^{.2} \;=\; .488$$

Note: We could also have done this using the marginal for X. The calculations are essentially the same as above.

10-44   Recall that to obtain the marginal density for Y we integrate the joint density with respect to x.

$$g_Y(y) \;=\; \int_{-\infty}^{\infty} f(x,y)\,dx$$

In order to set the limits of integration properly we will look at a graph showing the region where the joint density is positive.

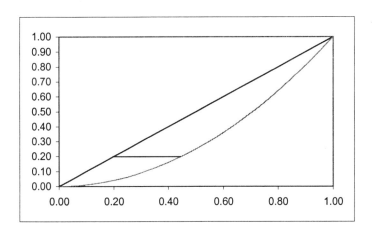

The region is bounded below by $y=x^2$ and above by $y=x$. However when we integrate with respect to x, we think of it as bounded on the left (below) by $x=y$ and on the right (above) by

$x = \sqrt{y}$ as indicated by the horizontal line inserted between the two curves. Thus for any y, $0 < y < 1$, we obtain the marginal $g(y)$ by the following integration.

$$g_Y(y) = \int_0^\infty f(x,y)\,dx$$
$$= \int_y^{\sqrt{y}} 15y\,dx = 15yx\Big|_{x=y}^{x=\sqrt{y}}$$
$$= 15y^{3/2} - 15y^2$$
$$= 15y^{3/2}(1 - y^{1/2})$$

10-45. We are asked to find $P(Y > .5)$. We will first find the complementary probability $P(Y < .5) = \iint_A f(x,y)\,dydx$, where A is the region filled in the graph below.

$$A = \{(x,y)\,|\,y \le .5 \,\&\, 0 \le x \le y\}.$$

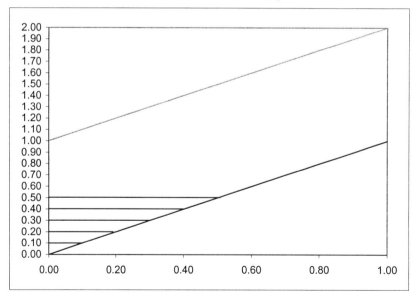

We are not directly given $f(x,y)$. However we can reconstruct it since were are told that:

(a) $f_X(x) = 1$ for $0 < x < 1$ from the statement "damage to the policyholder's car, X, has a marginal density function of 1 for $0 < x < 1$."

(b) $f(y|x) = 1$ for $x < y < x+1$ from the statement "Given $X = x$, the size of the payment for damage to the other driver's car, Y, has conditional density of 1 for $x < y < x+1$."

This tells us that

$$f(x,y) = f(x|y)f_X(x) = 1 \quad \text{for } 0 < x < 1 \text{ and } x < y < x+1.$$

We can avoid integrating since the joint density is constant.

$$P(Y < .5) = \iint_A f(x,y)dydx = 1(\text{area of A}) = \frac{.5^2}{2} = \frac{1}{8} \rightarrow$$
$$P(Y > .5) = 1 - \frac{1}{8} = \frac{7}{8}$$

10-46. We are asked to find $P(Y \geq 3) = \iint_A f(x,y)\, dydx$, where A is the region filled in the graph below.

$$A = \{(x,y) \mid 3 \leq y \leq 2x \ \& \ 1.5 \leq x \leq 2\}$$

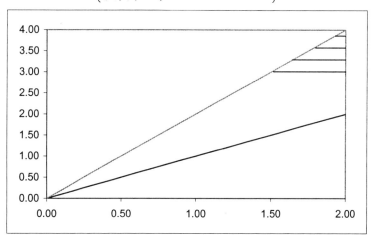

As in the previous problem, we are not directly given $f(x, y)$. However we can reconstruct it since were are told that:

(a) $f_X(x)$ is the density given in the problem above as $f(x)$.

(b) $f(y|x) = \frac{1}{x}$ for $x \le y \le 2x$ from the statement "The time (in hours) to process a claim of size x, where $0 \le x \le 2$, is uniformly distributed on the interval from x to $2x$."

This tells us that

$$f(x, y) = f(x|y) f_X(x) = \frac{3x}{8} \text{ for } 0 \le x \le 2 \text{ and } x \le y \le 2x.$$

$$
\begin{aligned}
P(Y \ge 3) &= \iint_A f(x, y) \, dy dx \\
&= \int_{1.5}^{2} \int_{3}^{2x} \frac{3}{8} x \, dy \, dx \\
&= \int_{1.5}^{2} \frac{3xy}{8} \bigg|_{3}^{2x} dx \\
&= \int_{1.5}^{2} \left(\frac{3x^2}{4} - \frac{9x}{8} \right) dx \\
&= \left(\frac{x^3}{4} - \frac{9x^2}{16} \right) \bigg|_{1.5}^{2} \\
&= .172
\end{aligned}
$$

10-47. First we will find the marginal density for X.

$$f_X(x) = \int_0^1 \frac{1}{64}(10 - xy^2) \, dy = \frac{1}{64}\left(10y - \frac{xy^3}{3} \right) \bigg|_0^1 = \frac{1}{64}\left(10 - \frac{x}{3} \right)$$

We are asked to find

$$
\begin{aligned}
E(X) &= \int_2^{10} x \frac{1}{64}\left(10 - \frac{x}{3} \right) dx = \int_2^{10} \frac{1}{64}\left(10x - \frac{x^2}{3} \right) dx \\
&= \frac{1}{64}\left(5x^2 - \frac{x^3}{9} \right) \bigg|_2^{10} = 5.78
\end{aligned}
$$

10-48. This problem must be read carefully. In many familiar probability problems X and Y represent the separate individual lifetimes of the two components. Here X represents the lifetime of the first component and Y represents the later time at which the second device fails. For example, the pair $X=8, Y=12$ means that the first device lasted 8 time units and the second lasted 4, so that the second device and the entire system failed at time 12.

We will review a useful fact from Chapter 8, Equation (8.7) that is helpful in this problem.

$$\int_0^\infty x^n e^{-ax}\, dx = \frac{n!}{a^{n+1}}$$

The special case that will occur in this problem is

$$\int_0^\infty x e^{-ax}\, dx = \frac{1}{a^2}$$

Knowing this will save you an integration by parts. You could also derive it if you remember the mean of the exponential random variable with parameter λ.

$$E(X) = \int_0^\infty x\lambda e^{-\lambda x}\, dx = \frac{1}{\lambda}$$

Now back to the problem. You are asked to find $E(Y)$. First we need to obtain the marginal distribution function $f_Y(y)$ by integrating the joint density function with respect to x. Note that the restriction $0 < x < y$ for the joint density will cause the limits of integration to be 0 and y.

$$f_Y(y) = \int_0^y f(x,y)\, dx = \int_0^y 6e^{-x}e^{-2y}\, dx$$

$$= (-6e^{-x}e^{-2y})\Big|_0^y = 6(e^{-2y} - e^{-3y})$$

$$E(Y) = \int_0^\infty 6y(e^{-2y} - e^{-3y})\, dy$$

$$= 6\left[\int_0^\infty y(e^{-2y})\, dy - \int_0^\infty y(e^{-3y})\, dy\right]$$

$$= 6\left[\frac{1}{2^2} - \frac{1}{3^2}\right] = .833$$

10-49. This is a Bayes Theorem problem, but it is based on a conditional distribution –you are given that the automobile was from one of the model years 1997, 1998, and 1999. This is equivalent to saying that the automobile was not in the Other class. Note that $P(\sim \text{Other}) = 1 - .46 = .54$. The conditional probabilities we need are

$$P(1997 \mid \sim \text{Other}) = \frac{P(1997 \& \sim \text{Other})}{P(\sim \text{Other})}$$

$$= \frac{P(1997)}{P(\sim \text{Other})} = \frac{.16}{.54} = .2963$$

$$P(1998 \mid \sim \text{Other}) = \frac{P(1998 \& \sim \text{Other})}{P(\sim \text{Other})}$$

$$= \frac{P(1998)}{P(\sim \text{Other})} = \frac{.18}{.54} = .3333$$

$$P(1999 \mid \sim \text{Other}) = \frac{P(1999 \& \sim \text{Other})}{P(\sim \text{Other})}$$

$$= \frac{P(1999)}{P(\sim \text{Other})} = \frac{.20}{.54} = .3704$$

Now we can do a standard Bayes Theorem tree.

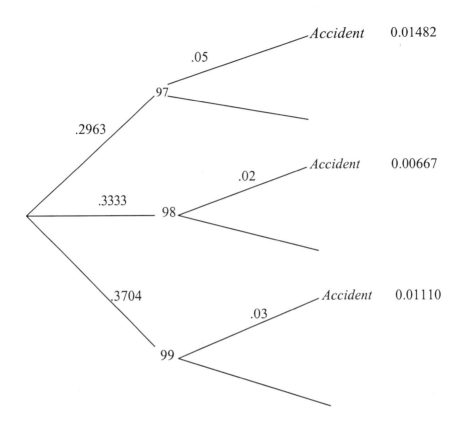

$$P(97 \mid \text{Accident}) \ = \ \frac{.01482}{.01482 + .00667 + .01110} \ = \ .45474$$

CHAPTER 11

11-1. If X and Y are the random variables in Exercise 10-1, the possible values of X are 1, 2 and 3, and of Y are 1 and 2. The possible values of $S = X+Y$ are 2, 3, 4 and 5. Since X and Y are independent,

$$p_S(s) = \sum_x p_X(x)p_Y(s-x).$$

$$p_S(2) = p_X(1)p_Y(1) = \left(\tfrac{2}{9}\right)\left(\tfrac{1}{3}\right) = \tfrac{2}{27}$$

$$p_S(3) = p_X(1)p_Y(2) + p_X(2)p_Y(1) = \left(\tfrac{2}{9}\right)\left(\tfrac{2}{3}\right) + \left(\tfrac{1}{3}\right)\left(\tfrac{1}{3}\right) = \tfrac{7}{27}$$

$$p_S(4) = p_X(2)p_Y(2) + p_X(3)p_Y(1) = \left(\tfrac{1}{3}\right)\left(\tfrac{2}{3}\right) + \left(\tfrac{4}{9}\right)\left(\tfrac{1}{3}\right) = \tfrac{10}{27}$$

$$p_S(5) = p_X(3)p_Y(2) = \left(\tfrac{4}{9}\right)\left(\tfrac{2}{3}\right) = \tfrac{8}{27}$$

11-2. If $f(x,y) = \left(\tfrac{4}{3}\right)(1-xy)$, $0 \le x \le 1$ and $0 \le y \le 1$:

$$
\begin{aligned}
P(X+Y \le 1) &= \int_0^1 \int_0^{1-y} f(x,y)\,dx\,dy \\
&= \int_0^1 \int_0^{1-y} \left(\tfrac{4}{3}\right)(1-xy)\,dx\,dy \\
&= \left(\tfrac{4}{3}\right)\int_0^1 \left(x - \tfrac{x^2 y}{2}\right)\Big|_{x=0}^{1-y}\,dy \\
&= \left(\tfrac{2}{3}\right)\int_0^1 (2 - 3y + 2y^2 - y^3)\,dy \\
&= \left(\tfrac{2}{3}\right)\left(2y - \tfrac{3y^2}{2} + \tfrac{2y^3}{3} - \tfrac{y^4}{4}\right)\Big|_0^1 \\
&= \tfrac{11}{18}
\end{aligned}
$$

11-3.   If $f_X(x) = 2e^{-2x}$ for $x > 0$ and $f_Y(y) = 3e^{-3y}$ for $y > 0$, and
$S = X + Y$:

$$f_S(s) = \int_{-\infty}^{\infty} f_X(x) f_Y(s-x)\, dx$$

$$= 6 \int_0^s e^{-2x} e^{-3(s-x)}\, dx$$

$$= 6e^{-3s} \int_0^s e^x\, dx = 6e^{-3s}(e^s - 1) = 6(e^{-2s} - e^{-3s}),\ s > 0$$

11-4.   From Example 11.3, $f(x,y) = 1 - 1.2x - .8y,\ 0 \le x \le 1,\ 0 \le y \le 1$.

$$P(X+Y \le 1.5) = 1 - P(X+Y > 1.5)$$

$$P(X+Y > 1.5) = \int_{.5}^{1} \int_{1.5-y}^{1} (2 - 1.2x - .8y)\, dxdy$$

$$= \int_{.5}^{1} (2x - .6x^2 - .8xy)\Big|_{x=1.5-y}^{1}\, dy$$

$$= \int_{.5}^{1} (-.25 + .6y - .2y^2)\, dy$$

$$= \left(-.25y + .3y^2 - \frac{.2y^3}{3}\right)\Big|_{.5}^{1} = .041\overline{6}$$

$$P(X+Y \le 1.5) = 1 - .041\overline{6} = .9583\overline{3}$$

11-5.   From Example 11.4, $f(x,y) - e^{-(x+y)},\ x \ge 0,\ y \ge 0$.
If $S = X + Y$:

$$F_S(s) = P(S \le s) = P(X+Y \le s)$$

$$= \int_0^s \int_0^{s-y} e^{-(x+y)}\, dxdy$$

$$= \int_0^s e^{s-y}(-e^{-x})\Big|_{x=0}^{s-y}\, dy$$

$$= \int_0^s (e^{-y} - e^{-s})\, dy$$

$$= (-e^{-y} - ye^{-s})\Big|_0^s = 1 - e^{-s}(1+s)$$

To compare $f_S(s)$ with Example 11.4,

$$f_S(s) = F_S'(s) = e^{-s} - e^{-s} + se^{-s} = se^{-s}.$$

11-6.   For the independent random variables in Exercise 10-6, we found that $f_X(x) = \frac{1}{2} + x$, for $0 \le x \le 1$, and $f_Y(y) = \frac{1}{2} + y$, for $0 \le y \le 1$.

$$P\big(\min(X,Y)\big) > t = P(X > t \text{ and } Y > t)$$

$$= P(X > t)P(Y > t)$$

$$= \left(\int_t^1 \left(\tfrac{1}{2} + x\right) dx \right)\left(\int_t^1 \left(\tfrac{1}{2} + y\right) dy \right)$$

(Note that both integrals give the same value)

$$= \left[\left(\tfrac{x}{2} + \tfrac{x^2}{2}\right)\Big|_t^1 \right]^2$$

$$= \left(1 - \tfrac{t}{2} - \tfrac{t^2}{2} \right)^2$$

11-7.   Using the table obtained in Exercise 10-1:

$$E(X+Y) = \sum_y \sum_x (x+y)p(x,y)$$

$$= (1+1)\left(\tfrac{2}{27}\right) + (2+1)\left(\tfrac{3}{27}\right) + (3+1)\left(\tfrac{4}{27}\right)$$

$$\quad + (1+2)\left(\tfrac{4}{27}\right) + (2+2)\left(\tfrac{6}{27}\right) + (2+3)\left(\tfrac{8}{27}\right)$$

$$= \tfrac{105}{27} = \tfrac{35}{9}$$

Using the probability distribution $f_S(s)$ from Exercise 11-1:

$$E(S) = E(X+Y) = \sum_s sf_S(s)$$

$$= 2\left(\tfrac{2}{27}\right) + 3\left(\tfrac{7}{27}\right) + 4\left(\tfrac{10}{27}\right) + 5\left(\tfrac{8}{27}\right) = \tfrac{35}{9}.$$

From Exercise 10-3, $E(X) = \tfrac{20}{9}$ and $E(Y) = \tfrac{5}{3} = \tfrac{15}{9}$, so

$$E(X) + E(Y) = \tfrac{20}{9} + \tfrac{15}{9} = \tfrac{35}{9} = E(X+Y).$$

11-8. For the joint density function $f(x,y)=\left(\frac{4}{3}\right)(1-xy),\ 0\le x\le 1,$ and $0\le y\le 1$:

$$E(X+Y) = \int_0^1 \int_0^1 (x+y)f(x,y)\,dxdy$$

$$= \left(\frac{4}{3}\right)\int_0^1 \int_0^1 (x+y-x^2y-xy^2)\,dxdy$$

$$= \left(\frac{4}{3}\right)\int_0^1 \left(\frac{x^2}{2}+xy-\frac{x^3y}{3}-\frac{x^2y^2}{2}\right)\Big|_{x=0}^{1}\,dy$$

$$= \left(\frac{4}{3}\right)\int_0^1 \left(\frac{1}{2}+\frac{2y}{3}-\frac{y^2}{2}\right)dy$$

$$= \left(\frac{4}{3}\right)\left(\frac{y}{2}+\frac{y^2}{3}-\frac{y^3}{6}\right)\Big|_0^1 = \frac{16}{18} = \frac{8}{9}$$

$$f_X(x) = \int_0^1 f(x,y)\,dy = \left(\frac{4}{3}\right)\int_0^1 (1-xy)\,dy$$

$$= \left(\frac{4}{3}\right)\left(y-\frac{xy^2}{2}\right)\Big|_{y=0}^{1} = \left(\frac{4}{3}\right)\left(1-\frac{x}{2}\right)$$

$$E(X) = \int_0^1 xf(x)\,dx = \left(\frac{4}{3}\right)\int_0^1 \left(x-\frac{x^2}{2}\right)dx$$

$$= \left(\frac{4}{3}\right)\left(\frac{x^2}{2}-\frac{x^3}{6}\right)\Big|_0^1 = \frac{4}{9}$$

A similar calculation will show that $E(Y)=\frac{4}{9}$,
so $E(X+Y) = E(X)+E(Y)$.

11-9. Let X and Y be random variables with joint density function $f(x,y)$.

$$E(X+Y) = \int_{-\infty}^{\infty}\int_{-\infty}^{\infty}(x+y)f(x,y)\,dx\,dy$$

$$= \int_{-\infty}^{\infty}x\int_{-\infty}^{\infty}f(x,y)\,dydx + \int_{-\infty}^{\infty}y\int_{-\infty}^{\infty}f(x,y)\,dxdy$$

$$= \int_{-\infty}^{\infty}xf_X(x)\,dx + \int_{-\infty}^{\infty}yf_Y(y)\,dy$$

$$= E(X)+E(Y)$$

11-10. For the random variables (independent) in Example 11.9:

$$E(XY) = \sum_y \sum_x xyp(x,y) = \sum_y \sum_x xyp_X(x)p_Y(y)$$

The only non-zero terms occur when both $x \neq 0$ and $y \neq 0$, i.e. when $(x,y) = (1,1), (1,2), (2,1)$ or $(2,2)$.

$$E(XY) = 1\left(\tfrac{1}{4}\right)\left(\tfrac{1}{4}\right) + 2\left(\tfrac{1}{4}\right)\left(\tfrac{1}{4}\right) + 2\left(\tfrac{1}{4}\right)\left(\tfrac{1}{4}\right) + 4\left(\tfrac{1}{4}\right)\left(\tfrac{1}{4}\right) = \tfrac{9}{16}$$

11-11. For the random variables in Exercise 11-8, $f(x,y) = \left(\tfrac{4}{3}\right)(1-xy)$, for $0 \leq x \leq 1$ and $0 \leq y \leq 1$.

(a) $E(XY) = \displaystyle\int_0^1 \int_0^1 xyf(x,y)\, dx\, dy$

$$= \left(\tfrac{4}{3}\right)\int_0^1 \int_0^1 (xy - x^2 y^2)\, dx\, dy = \left(\tfrac{4}{3}\right)\int_0^1 \left(\tfrac{x^2 y}{2} - \tfrac{x^3 y^2}{3}\right)\Big|_{x=0}^{1} dy$$

$$= \left(\tfrac{4}{3}\right)\int_0^1 \left(\tfrac{y}{2} - \tfrac{y^2}{3}\right) dy = \left(\tfrac{4}{3}\right)\left(\tfrac{y^2}{4} - \tfrac{y^3}{9}\right)\Big|_0^1 = \left(\tfrac{4}{3}\right)\left(\tfrac{5}{36}\right) = \tfrac{5}{27}$$

(b) $E(X) = E(Y) = \tfrac{4}{9}$ from Exercise 11-8, so $E(X)E(Y) = \tfrac{16}{81}$

(c) $Cov(X,Y) = E(XY) - E(X)E(Y) = \tfrac{5}{27} - \tfrac{16}{81} = -\tfrac{1}{81}$

11-12. For the random variables in Exercise 11-8:

(a) $f_X(x) = \left(\tfrac{4}{3}\right)\left(1 - \tfrac{x}{2}\right)$, for $0 \leq x \leq 1$

$$E(X^2) = \int_0^1 x^2 f_X(x)\, dx$$

$$= \left(\tfrac{4}{3}\right)\int_0^1 \left(x^2 - \tfrac{x^3}{2}\right) dx$$

$$= \left(\tfrac{4}{3}\right)\left(\tfrac{x^3}{3} - \tfrac{x^4}{8}\right)\Big|_0^1 = \left(\tfrac{4}{3}\right)\left(\tfrac{5}{24}\right) = \tfrac{5}{18}$$

$$V(X) = E(X^2) - E(X)^2 = \tfrac{5}{18} - \tfrac{16}{81} = \tfrac{13}{162}$$

(b) A similar calculation will show $V(Y) = \tfrac{13}{162}$.

(c) $V(X+Y) = V(X) + V(Y) + 2Cov(X,Y) = \tfrac{13}{162} + \tfrac{13}{162} - \tfrac{2}{81} = \tfrac{11}{81}$

11-13. For the random variables in Exercise 10-1 we have already shown (see Exercise 10-3) that $E(X) = \frac{20}{9}$ and $E(Y) = \frac{5}{3}$.

$$E(X^2) = \sum_x x^2 p_X(x) = 1\left(\frac{2}{9}\right) + 4\left(\frac{1}{3}\right) + 9\left(\frac{4}{9}\right) = \frac{50}{9}$$

$$V(X) = E(X^2) - E(X)^2 = \frac{50}{9} - \left(\frac{20}{9}\right)^2 = \frac{50}{81}$$

$$E(Y^2) = \sum_y y^2 p_Y(y) = 1\left(\frac{1}{3}\right) + 4\left(\frac{2}{3}\right) = 3$$

$$V(Y) = E(Y^2) - E(Y)^2 = 3 - \left(\frac{5}{3}\right)^2 = \frac{2}{9}$$

Since X and Y are independent (see Exercise 10-23),

$$V(X+Y) = V(X) + V(Y) = \frac{50}{81} + \frac{2}{9} = \frac{68}{81}.$$

11-14. (a) $E(X) = 1(.5) + 2(.5) = 1.5$

(b) $E(Y) = 1(.4) + 2(.6) = 1.6$

(c) $E(X^2) = 1(.5) + 4(.5) = 2.5$
$V(X) = 2.5 - (1.5)^2 = .25$

(d) $E(Y^2) = 1(.4) + 4(.6) = 2.8$
$V(Y) = 2.8 - (1.6)^2 = .24$

(e) $E(XY) = 1(.15) + 2(.25) + 2(.35) + 4(.25) = 2.35$
$Cov(X,Y) = E(XY) - E(X)E(Y)$
$= 2.35 - (1.5)(1.6) = -.05$

(f) $V(X+Y) = V(X) + V(Y) + 2Cov(X,Y)$
$= .25 + .24 - .10 = .39$

11-15. For the random variables in Exercise 10-22, we have already shown $f_Y(y) = 3y^2$, for $0 \le y \le 1$.

$$f_X(x) = \int_x^1 f(x)\,dy = 6\int_x^1 x\,dy = 6x(1-x), \text{ for } 0 \le x \le 1$$

$$E(X) = \int_0^1 x(6x)(1-x)\,dx = 6\int_0^1 (x^2 - x^3)\,dx = 6\left(\frac{x^3}{3} - \frac{x^4}{4}\right)\Big|_0^1 = \frac{1}{2}$$

$$E(X^2) = \int_0^1 x^2(6x)(1-x)\,dx = 6\int_0^1 (x^3 - x^4)\,dx$$

$$= 6\left(\frac{x^4}{4} - \frac{x^5}{5}\right)\Big|_0^1 = \frac{3}{10}$$

$$E(Y) = \int_0^1 3y^3\,dy = \left(\frac{3y^4}{4}\right)\Big|_0^1 = \frac{3}{4}$$

$$E(Y^2) = \int_0^1 3y^4\,dy = \left(\frac{3y^5}{5}\right)\Big|_0^1 = \frac{3}{5}$$

(a) $V(X) = \frac{3}{10} - \left(\frac{1}{2}\right)^2 = \frac{1}{20}$

(b) $V(Y) = \frac{3}{5} - \left(\frac{3}{4}\right)^2 = \frac{3}{80}$

(c) $E(XY) = \int_0^1 \int_0^y xyf(x,y)\,dxdy$

$$= \int_0^1 \int_0^y 6x^2 y\,dxdy$$

$$= \int_0^1 (2x^3 y)\big|_{x=0}^{y}\,dy = \int_0^1 2y^4\,dy = \left(\frac{2y^2}{5}\right)\Big|_0^1 = \frac{2}{5}$$

(d) $Cov(X,Y) = E(XY) - E(X)E(Y) = \frac{2}{5} - \left(\frac{1}{2}\right)\left(\frac{3}{4}\right) = \frac{1}{40}$

$V(X+Y) = V(X) + V(Y) + 2Cov(X,Y) = \frac{1}{20} + \frac{3}{80} + \frac{2}{40} = \frac{11}{80}$

11-16. For the random variables in Exercise 11-14, $V(X) = .25$, $V(Y) = .24$ and $Cov(X < Y) = -.05$. Hence

$$\rho_{XY} = \frac{Cov(X,Y)}{\sqrt{V(X)V(Y)}} = \frac{-.05}{\sqrt{(.25)(.24)}} = -.2041$$

11-17. For the random variables in Exercise 11-15, $V(X) = \frac{1}{20}$,

$V(Y) = \frac{3}{80}$ and $Cov(X,Y) = \frac{1}{40}$. Hence

$$\rho_{XY} = \frac{Cov(X,Y)}{\sqrt{V(X)V(Y)}} = \frac{1/40}{\sqrt{(1/20)(3/80)}} = .5774.$$

11-18. Let X and Y be random variables whose joint density function is
$f(x,y) = x+y$, for $0 \le x \le 1$ and $0 < y \le 1$.

$$f_X(x) = \int_0^1 f(x,y)\,dy = \int_0^1 (x+y)\,dy$$

$$= \left(xy + \frac{y^2}{2}\right)\Big|_{y=0}^1 = x + \frac{1}{2}, \text{ for } 0 \le x \le 1$$

$$E(X) = \int_0^1 xf_X(x)dx = \int_0^1 \left(x^2 + \frac{x}{2}\right)dx = \left(\frac{x^3}{3} + \frac{x^2}{4}\right)\Big|_0^1 = \frac{7}{12}$$

$$E(X^2) = \int_0^1 x^2 f_X(x)dx = \int_0^1 \left(x^3 + \frac{x^2}{2}\right)dx = \left(\frac{x^4}{4} + \frac{x^3}{6}\right)\Big|_0^1 = \frac{5}{12}$$

$$V(X) = \frac{5}{12} - \left(\frac{7}{12}\right)^2 = \frac{11}{144}$$

A similar calculation will show that $E(Y) = \frac{7}{12}$ and $V(Y) = \frac{11}{144}$.

$$E(XY) = \int_0^1 \int_0^1 xy(x+y)\,dxdy$$

$$= \int_0^1 \int_0^1 (x^2y + xy^2)\,dxdy$$

$$= \int_0^1 \left(\frac{x^3y}{3} + \frac{x^2y^2}{2}\right)\Big|_{x=0}^1 dy = \int_0^1 \left(\frac{y}{3} + \frac{y^2}{2}\right)dy$$

$$= \left(\frac{1}{6}\right)(y^2 + y^3)\Big|_0^1 = \frac{1}{3}$$

$$Cov(X,Y) = E(XY) - E(X)E(Y) = \frac{1}{3} - \left(\frac{7}{12}\right)\left(\frac{7}{12}\right) = -\frac{1}{144}$$

$$\rho_{XY} = \frac{Cov(X,Y)}{\sqrt{V(X)V(Y)}} = \frac{-1/144}{\sqrt{(11/144)^2}} = -\frac{1}{11}$$

11-19. Let $f(x,y) = \left(\frac{3}{8}\right)(x^2+y^2)$, for $-1 \le x \le 1$ and $-1 \le y \le 1$.

(a) $f_x(x) = \left(\frac{3}{8}\right)\int_{-1}^{1}(x^2+y^2)\,dy$

$ = \left(\frac{3}{8}\right)\left(x^2 y + \frac{y^3}{3}\right)\Big|_{y=-1}^{1}$

$ = \left(\frac{3}{8}\right)\left(2x^2 + \frac{2}{3}\right) = \frac{3x^2}{4} + \frac{1}{4}$, for $-1 \le x \le 1$

$f_Y(y) = \left(\frac{3}{8}\right)\int_{-1}^{1}(x^2+y^2)\,dx = \frac{1}{4} + \frac{3y^2}{4}$, for $-1 \le y \le 1$

$f_X(x)f_Y(y) = \left(\frac{1}{4} + \frac{3x^2}{4}\right)\left(\frac{1}{4} + \frac{3y^2}{4}\right) \ne (x^2+y^2) = f(x,y)$

Hence X and Y are not independent.

(b) $E(X) = \int_{-1}^{1} x f_X(x)\,dx = \int_{-1}^{1}\left(\frac{x}{4} + \frac{3x^3}{4}\right)dx$

$ = \left(\frac{x^2}{8} + \frac{3x^4}{16}\right)\Big|_{-1}^{1} = 0$

By a similar calculation, $E(Y) = 0$.

$E(XY) = \int_{-1}^{1}\int_{-1}^{1} xy f(x,y)\,dx\,dy$

$ = \left(\frac{3}{8}\right)\int_{-1}^{1}\int_{-1}^{1} xy(x^2+y^2)\,dx\,dy$

$ = \left(\frac{3}{8}\right)\int_{-1}^{1}\left(\frac{x^4 y}{4} + \frac{x^2 y^3}{2}\right)\Big|_{x=-1}^{1} dy = 0$

$Cov(X,Y) = E(XY) - E(X)E(Y) = 0$

11-20.   The joint probability function yields the following table.

y \ x	1	2	$p_Y(y)$
1	$\frac{2}{15}$	$\frac{4}{15}$	$\frac{2}{5}$
2	$\frac{3}{15}$	$\frac{6}{15}$	$\frac{3}{5}$
$p_X(x)$	$\frac{1}{3}$	$\frac{2}{3}$	

X and Y are clearly independent.

$$M_X(t) = E(e^{tX}) = \sum_x e^{tx} p(x) = \left(\tfrac{1}{3}\right)e^t + \left(\tfrac{2}{3}\right)e^{2t}$$

$$M_Y(t) = E(e^{tY}) = \sum_y e^{ty} p(y) = \tfrac{2}{5}e^t + \left(\tfrac{3}{5}\right)e^{2t}$$

By independence:

$$M_{X+Y}(t) = M_X(t)M_Y(t) = \left(\tfrac{1}{15}\right)(2e^{2t} + 7e^{3t} + 6e^{4t})$$

11-21.   If X and y are each uniformly distributed over $[0, 2]$, then

$$M_X(t) = M_Y(t) = \frac{e^{2t}-1}{2t}. \text{ (Exercise 9-4)}$$

Since X and Y are independent,

$$M_{X+Y}(t) = M_X(t)M_Y(t) = \frac{(e^{2t}-1)^2}{4t^2}.$$

11-22.   By Example 5.25 and Exercise 5-33, for each i, $E(X_i) = \tfrac{7}{2}$ and $V(X_i) = \tfrac{35}{12}$.

$$E(S) = E(X_1) + E(X_2) + \cdots + E(X_n) = n\left(\tfrac{7}{2}\right)$$

Since the X_i's are independent,

$$V(S) = V(X_1) + V(X_2) + \cdots + V(X_n) = n\left(\tfrac{35}{12}\right).$$

11-23. $$V(X_1 + X_2 + X_3 + X_4) = \sum_{i=1}^{4} V(X_i) + 2\sum_{i<j} Cov(X_i X_j)$$

$$= 4\left(\tfrac{13}{162}\right) + 2(6)\left(-\tfrac{1}{81}\right) = \tfrac{14}{81}$$

11-24. If $S = X_1 + X_2 + \cdots + X_{10}, V(S) = \frac{500}{9}, V(X_i) = \frac{25}{3}$ for each i, and all covariances $Cov(X_i, X_j)$ for $i \neq j$ are the same, then

$$V(S) = \sum_{i=1}^{10} V(X_i) + 2\sum_{i<j} Cov(X_i, X_j).$$

(The number of terms in the covariance sum is $1 + 2 + \cdots + 9 = 45$.)

$$\frac{500}{9} = 10\left(\frac{25}{3}\right) + 2(45)Cov(X_i, X_j)$$
$$Cov(X_i, X_j) = -\frac{25}{81}$$

11-25. S is the sum of 500 independent and identically distributed random variables each with mean .50 and variance .25. Then S is approximately normal with $\mu = 500(.5)$ and $\sigma^2 = 500(.25)$.

$$P(235 \leq S \leq 265) = P\left(\frac{235 - 250}{\sqrt{125}} \leq Z \leq \frac{265 - 250}{\sqrt{125}}\right)$$
$$= P(-1.34 \leq Z \leq 1.34) = .8198$$

For Exercises 11-26 to 11-30, we make the following table of conditional probabilities from the table in Example 11.30, e.g.,

$$p(0|90) = P(Y = 0 | X = 90) = \frac{p(90, 0)}{p_X(90)} = \frac{.05}{.20} = .25.$$

y	0	10
$p(y\|90)$	.25	.75
$p(y\|100)$	.45	.55
$p(y\|110)$	.90	.10

11-26. (a) $E(Y|X = 90) = 0p(0|90) + 10p(10|90) = 0 + 7.5 = 7.5$

(b) $E(Y|X=100) = 0p(0|100) + 10p(10|100) = 5.5$

(c) $E(Y|X=110) = 0p(0|110) + 10p(10|110) = 1$

11-27. $E[E(Y|X)] = E(Y|X{=}90)p_X(90) + E(Y|X{=}100)p_X(100)$
$$+E(Y|X{=}110)p_X(100)$$
$$= 7.5(.20) + 5.5(.60) + 1(.20) = 5 = E(Y)$$

11-28. (a) $E(Y^2|X{=}90) = 0(.25) + 100(.75) = 75$
$V(Y|X{=}90) = 75 - (7.5)^2 = 18.75$

(b) $E(Y^2|X{=}100) = 0(.45) + 10(.55) = 55$
$V(Y|X{=}100) = 55 - (5.5)^2 = 24.75$

(c) $E(Y^2|X{=}110) = 0(.90) + 100(.10) = 10$
$V(Y|X{=}110) = 10 - 1 = 9$

11-29. $E[V(Y|X)] = V(Y|X{=}90)p_X(90)$
$$+V(Y|X{=}100)p_Y(100) + V(Y|X{=}110)p_X(110)$$
$$= 18.75(.20) + 24.75(.60) + 9(.20) = 20.4$$

11-30. $V[E(Y|X)] = \sum_x \left(E(Y|X = x) - E(Y) \right)^2 p_X(x)$
$$= (7.5{-}5)^2(.2) + (5.5 - 5)^2(.6) + (1 - 5)^2(.2)$$
$$= 4.6$$

$V[E(Y|X)] + E[V(Y|X)] = 4.6 + 20.4 = 25 = V(Y)$

11-31. Let S be the random variable indicating whether a claim has been filed (S=1) or not (S=0). Then $P(S=0) = .93$ and $P(S=1) = .07$. Let X be the random variable of the claim amount paid.

$$P(X = 500 \,|\, S = 1) = .60$$
$$P(X = 1000 \,|\, S = 1) = .30$$
$$P(X = 2000 \,|\, S = 1) = .10$$

$$E(X \,|\, S = 0) = 0 \text{ and } V(X \,|\, S = 0) = 0$$

$$E(X \,|\, S = 1) = 500(.60) + 1000(.30) + 2000(.10) = 800$$
$$E[E(X \,|\, S)] = E(X) = 0(.93) + 800(.07) = 56$$

$$E(X^2 \,|\, S = 1) = 500^2(.60) + 1000^2(.30) + 2000^2(.10) = 850,000$$
$$V(X \,|\, S = 1) = 850,000 - 800^2 = 210,000$$
$$E[V(X \,|\, S)] = 0(.93) + 210,000(.07) = 14,700$$

$$V[E(X \,|\, S)] = \left(E(X \,|\, S = 0) - E(X)\right)^2 P(S = 0)$$
$$+ \left(E(X \,|\, S = 1) - E(X)\right)^2 P(S = 1)$$
$$= (0 - 56)^2(.93) + (800 - 56)^2(.07) = 41,664$$

$$V(X) = V[E(X \,|\, S)] + E[V(X \,|\, S)] = 41,664 + 14,700$$
$$= 56,364$$

11-32. For $f(x,y) = 6x$, $0 < x < y < 1$ and 0 elsewhere:

(a) $f_X(x) = \int_x^1 6x\,dy = 6x(1-x)\,dx$, for $0 < x < 1$

(b) $E(X) = \int_0^1 (6x^2 - 6x^3)\,dx = \frac{1}{2}$

(c) $E(X^2) = \int_0^1 (6x^3 - 6x^4)\,dx = \frac{3}{10}$

$$V(X) = \frac{3}{10} - \left(\frac{1}{2}\right)^2 = \frac{1}{20}$$

(Note: All these were calculated in Exercise 11-15.)

11-33. In Exercise 10-22 we showed that $f_Y(y) = 3y^2,\ 0 < y < 1$.

$$f(x\mid y) = \frac{f(x,y)}{f_Y(y)} = \frac{6x}{3y^2} = \frac{2x}{y^2},\ 0 < x < y$$

$$E(X\mid Y=y) = \int_0^y xf(x\mid y)dx$$

$$= \int_0^y \frac{2x^2}{y^2}dx = \frac{2x^3}{3y^2}\Big|_{x=0}^y = \frac{2y}{3}$$

$$E[E(X\mid Y)] = \int_0^1 E(X\mid Y=y)f_Y(y)dy$$

$$= \int_0^1 \frac{2y}{3}(3y^2)\,dy = \left(\frac{2y^4}{4}\right)\Big|_0^1 = \frac{1}{2}\ \text{(This equals } E(X)\text{.)}$$

11-34. $$E(X^2\mid Y=y) = \int_0^y x^2\left(\frac{2x}{y^2}\right)dx = \frac{2x^4}{4y^2}\Big|_0^y = \frac{y^2}{2}$$

$$V(X\mid Y=y) = \frac{y^2}{2} - \left(\frac{2y}{3}\right)^2 = \frac{y^2}{18}$$

11-35. $$E[V(X\mid Y)] = \int_0^1 V(X\mid Y=y)f_Y(y)\,dy = \int_0^1 \frac{y^4}{6}\,dy = \frac{y^5}{30}\Big|_0^1 = \frac{1}{30}$$

11-36. $$E[E(X\mid Y)^2] = \int_0^1 \left(\frac{2y}{3}\right)^2 (3y^2)\,dy = \frac{4y^5}{15}\Big|_0^1 = \frac{4}{15}$$

$$V[E(X\mid Y)] = \frac{4}{15} - \left(\frac{1}{2}\right)^2 = \frac{1}{60}$$

$$E[V(X\mid Y)] + V[E(X\mid Y)] = \frac{1}{30} + \frac{1}{60} = \frac{1}{20} = V(X)$$

11-37. The number of claims N is a Poisson random variable, so $E(N) = V(N) = \lambda = 20$. The amounts of claim random variable X is uniform over $[0,\ 500]$, so $E(X) = 250$ and $V(X) = \frac{500^2}{12}$.

(a) $E(S) = E(N)E(X) = 20(250) = 5000$

(b) $V(S) = E(N)V(X) + V(N)E(X)^2$
       $$= 20\left(\frac{500^2}{12} + 250^2\right) = 1{,}666{,}666.67$$

11-38. If the amount of claim random variable X is lognormal whose underlying normal distribution has $\mu = 5$ and $\sigma = .40$:

$$E(X) = e^{\mu + \frac{\sigma^2}{2}} = e^{5.08}$$

$$V(X) \;=\; e^{2\mu + \sigma^2}(e^{\sigma^2} - 1) \;=\; e^{10.16}(e^{.16} - 1)$$

(a) $E(S) = 20e^{5.08} = 3215.48$

(b) $V(S) \;=\; 20[e^{10.16}(e^{.16} - 1) + e^{10.16}) \;=\; 606,665.15$

11-39. The claim amount S is approximately normal, with

$$\mu \;=\; E(N)E(X) \;=\; 500(250) \;=\; 125,000$$

and

$$\sigma^2 \;=\; 500\!\left(\tfrac{500^2}{12} + 250^2\right)\!, \text{ so } \sigma \;=\; 6454.97.$$

$$P(S \le 140,000) \;=\; P\!\left(Z \le \tfrac{140,000 - 125,000}{6454.97}\right)$$
$$=\; P(Z \le 2.32) \;=\; .9898$$

11-40. If $E(X) = 600$ and $V(X) = 12,000$, then S is approximately normal with $\mu = 500(600) = 300,000$ and

$$\sigma^2 \;=\; 500(12,000 + 600^2), \text{ so } = 13,638.18.$$

We need to find S_0 so that $P(S \le S_0) = .95$. From the z-tables we know that $F_Z(1.645) \approx .95$. Hence

$$P(Z \le 1.645) \;=\; P\!\left(\tfrac{S - 300,000}{13,638.18} \le 1.645\right) \approx .95.$$

Therefore $S_0 \;=\; 300,000 + 1.645(13,638.18) \;=\; 322,434.81.$

11-41. Let N_1 and N_2 be the numbers of claims for the first and second weeks of a two-week period. For a two week period we must find the probability of each pair (n_1, n_2) for which $n_1 + n_2 = 7$ and sum those probabilities. We can write this simply as

$$p(0,7) + p(1,6) + \cdots + p(7,0) = \sum_{i=0}^{7} p(i, 7-i)$$

Note that by independence, for each pair in the sum above

$$p(i, 7-i) = p(i)p(7-i) = \left(\frac{1}{2^{i+1}}\right)\left(\frac{1}{2^{7-i+1}}\right) = \frac{1}{2^9}$$

The number of terms in the sum above is $8 = 2^3$. Thus the sum is

$$8\left(\frac{1}{2^9}\right) = \frac{1}{2^6} = \frac{1}{64}$$

11-42. Let X_1, X_2, X_3, X_4 be the random variables for the 4 bids. The bid accepted will be $Max = \max(X_1, X_2, X_3, X_4)$. The cumulative distribution for the bid accepted will be

$$F_{Max}(x) = F_{X_1}(x)F_{X_2}(x)F_{X_3}(x)F_{X_4}(x)$$
$$= (F(x))^4 = \frac{1}{16}(1 + \sin \pi x)^4 \quad \text{for } \frac{3}{2} \le x \le \frac{5}{2}$$

The density function for the bid accepted will be

$$f_{Max}(x) = \frac{d}{dx}F_{Max}(x)$$
$$= \frac{d}{dx}\frac{1}{16}(1 + \sin \pi x)^4$$
$$= \frac{1}{4}\pi\cos\pi x(1+\sin\pi x)^3 \quad \text{for } \frac{3}{2} \le x \le \frac{5}{2}$$

Now we can integrate to get the expected value.

$$E[Max] = \int_{3/2}^{5/2} xf_{Max}(x)\,dx = \frac{1}{4}\pi \int_{3/2}^{5/2} x\cos\pi x(1+\sin\pi x)^3\,dx$$

11-43. Let X_1, X_2, X_3 be the random variables for the 3 independent claims. We need to find the expected value of $Max = \max(X_1, X_2, X_3)$. The cumulative distribution for the largest claim will be

$$F_{Max}(x) = F_{X_1}(x_1)F_{X_2}(x_2)F_{X_3}(x_3) = \left(F(x)\right)^3.$$

We must calculate the common cumulative distribution function $F(x)$.

$$F(x) = \int_0^x 3u^{-4}\,du = \left. -u^{-3}\right|_1^x = 1-\frac{1}{x^3} \quad \text{for } x>1.$$

Thus

$$F_{Max}(x) = \left(F(x)\right)^3 = \left(1-\frac{1}{x^3}\right)^3 \qquad \text{for } x>1$$

$$f_{Max}(x) = \frac{d}{dx}F_{Max}(x) = \frac{d}{dx}\left[\left(1-\frac{1}{x^3}\right)^3\right]$$

$$= \frac{9}{x^4}\left(1-\frac{1}{x^3}\right)^2$$

$$= \left(\frac{9}{x^4}-\frac{18}{x^7}+\frac{9}{x^{10}}\right) \text{ for } x>1$$

Now we can integrate to get the expected value (in thousands).

$$E[Max] = \int_1^\infty xf_{Max}(x)\,dx$$

$$= \int_1^\infty x\left(\frac{9}{x^4}-\frac{18}{x^7}+\frac{9}{x^{10}}\right)dx$$

$$= \int_1^\infty (9x^{-3}-18x^{-6}+9x^{-9})\,dx$$

$$= \left. \left(-\frac{9}{2}x^{-2}+\frac{18}{5}x^{-5}-\frac{9}{8}x^{-8}\right)\right|_1^\infty$$

$$= 2.025$$

Multiplying by 1000, we get expected value of 2025.

11-44. We need to find $P(X+Y \geq 1) = 1 - P(X+Y < 1)$. If we look at the diagram of the regions involved, we see that the second approach involves less integration.

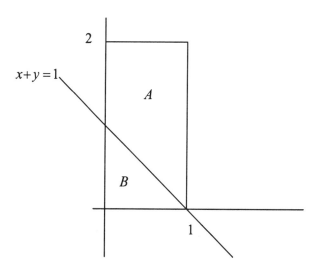

$$P(X+Y \geq 1) = 1 - P(X+Y < 1)$$

$$= 1 - \iint_B f(x,y)\, dydx$$

$$= 1 - \tfrac{1}{4} \int_0^1 \int_0^{1-x} (2x-2-y)\, dydx$$

$$= 1 - .29$$

$$= .71$$

11-45. Let X and Y be the random variables for the losses on the policies with deductibles of 1 and 2 respectively. Note that X and Y are independent, each with density function $f(x) = \frac{1}{10}$ for $0 \le x \le 10$.

Thus the joint distribution function is $f(x,y) = \left(\frac{1}{10}\right)^2 = \frac{1}{100}$ for $0 \le x \le 10$ and $0 \le y \le 10$.

The benefit paid after deductible is $X - 1$ for the first policy and $Y - 2$ for the second. In order for the total benefit to be less than or equal to 5, we need to satisfy the conditions $X - 1 \le 5$, $Y - 2 \le 5$ and $X - 1 + Y - 2 \le 5$. This is equivalent to $X \le 6$, $Y \le 7$ and $X + Y \le 8$. The region A on which these conditions are satisfied is indicated in the diagram below.

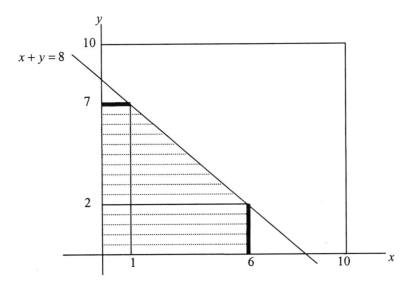

Since $f(x,y) = \frac{1}{100}$ is constant we can avoid integrating. The desired probability is

$$\iint_A f(x,y)\, dy\, dx = \left(\frac{1}{100}\right)(\text{area of } A)$$

The area of A can be written as the sum of the areas of two rectangles and a triangle, i.e., $7(1) + 2(5) + 5(5)/2 = 29.5$. Thus the desired probability is $\frac{29.5}{100} = .295$.

11-46. The region R over which $f(t_1,t_2)$, is constant is pictured below.

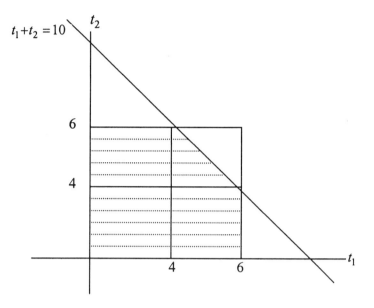

The area of the region is 34, so we must have $f(t_1,t_2)=\frac{1}{34}$ over the region in order to guarantee that $\iint_R f(t_1,t_2)\ dt_1\ dt_2 = 1$. We need to find

$$E[T_1+T_2] = \iint_R (t_1+t_2)\left(\tfrac{1}{34}\right)dt_2\ dt_1$$

$$= \tfrac{1}{34}\left[\int_0^4\int_0^6 (t_1+t_2)\ dt_2\ dt_1 + \int_4^6\int_0^{10-t_1}(t_1+t_2)\ dt_2\ dt_1\right]$$

$$= \tfrac{1}{34}\left[120+\tfrac{224}{3}\right] = 5.72$$

11-47   The region R where L is a positive constant is pictured below.

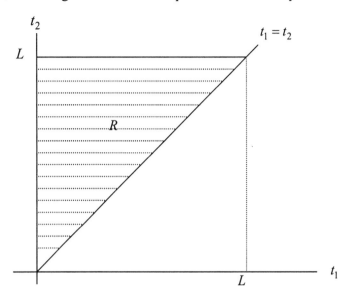

The area of the region is $\frac{L^2}{2}$, so we must have $f(t_1,t_2) = \frac{2}{L^2}$ over the region in order to guarantee that $\iint_R f(t_1,t_2)\, dt_1\, dt_2 = 1$. We need to find

$$
\begin{aligned}
E(T_1^2 + T_2^2) &= \iint_R \left[\left(t_1^2 + t_2^2 \right) \right] \left(\frac{2}{L^2} \right) dt_1\, dt_2 \\
&= \frac{2}{L^2} \int_0^L \int_0^{t_2} \left(t_1^2 + t_2^2 \right) dt_1\, dt_2 \\
&= \frac{2}{L^2} \int_0^L \left(\frac{t_1^3}{3} + t_1 t_2^2 \right) \Bigg|_0^{t_2} dt_2 \\
&= \frac{2}{L^2} \int_0^L \left(\frac{4 t_2^3}{3} \right) dt_2 \;=\; \frac{2}{L^2} \frac{t_1^4}{3} \Bigg|_0^L \;=\; \frac{2L^2}{3}
\end{aligned}
$$

11-48 Let X_1, X_2, X_3 be the random variables for the losses due to storm, fire and theft respectively. We need to find $P[Max > 3]$, where $Max = \max(X_1, X_2, X_3)$. The cumulative distribution will be

$$F_{Max}(t) = F_{X_1}(t)F_{X_2}(t)F_{X_3}(t) = (1-e^{-x})(1-e^{-x/1.5})(1-e^{-x/2.4}).$$

Then

$$P(Max \le 3) = F_{Max}(3) = (1-e^{-3})(1-e^{-3/1.5})(1-e^{-3/2.4}) = .586$$

$$P[Max > 3] = 1 - .586 = .414$$

11-49. Let Y and Z be the independent exponential random variables for claims and premiums. Then $f_Y(y) = e^{-y}$ and $f_Z(z) = 0.5e^{-0.5z}$. We are asked to find the density function of $X = Y/Z$. Note that the joint density function for Y and Z is $f(z,y) = (0.5e^{-0.5z})e^{-y}$.

We will first find the cumulative distribution for X, i.e., we will calculate $F_X(x)$ for an arbitrary value of $x > 0$. First note that

$$F_X(x) = P(X \le x)$$
$$= P\left(\frac{Y}{Z} \le x\right)$$
$$= P(Y \le Zx)$$

The region of integration for this probability is the first quadrant area bounded by the line $y = zx$ and the z-axis.

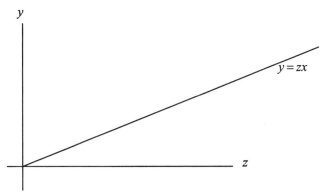

For any fixed value of $x > 0$, we can calculate $F_X(x)$ as

$$P(Y \le Zx) = \int_0^\infty \int_0^{zx} f(z,y)\, dy\, dz$$

$$= .5 \int_0^\infty (e^{-0.5z}) \left(\int_0^{zx} e^{-y}\, dy \right) dz$$

$$= .5 \int_0^\infty (e^{-0.5z})(1 - e^{-zx})\, dz$$

$$= .5 \int_0^\infty (e^{-0.5z} - e^{-z(x+0.5)})\, dz$$

$$= .5 \left(\frac{e^{-0.5z}}{-0.5} - \frac{e^{-z(x+0.5)}}{-(x+0.5)} \right) \Bigg|_0^\infty$$

$$= 1 - \frac{1}{2x+1}$$

$$f_X(x) = \frac{d}{dx} F_X(x)$$

$$= \frac{d}{dx} \left[1 - \frac{1}{2x+1} \right]$$

$$= \frac{2}{(2x+1)^2} \quad \text{for} \quad x > 0$$

11-50. We will look at the total hours for a single individual first, and then use the central limit theorem to finish the problem with a normal approximation.

For one individual, the total hours watching movies or sporting events is $S = X+Y$. The mean and variance of X are

$$E(S) = E(X+Y) = E(X)+E(Y) = 50+20 = 70$$

$$V(S) = V(X+Y) = V(X)+V(Y)+2Cov(X,Y)$$
$$= 50+30+2(10) = 100$$

The one hundred people were randomly selected, so we will assume that they are independent. The problem states that they all have the identical distribution given. The total for all 100 people is

$$T = S_1 + \cdots + S_{100}.$$

By the central limit theorem, T is approximately normal with

$$E(T) = \mu_T = 100(70) = 7,000$$
$$V(T) = \sigma_T^2 = 100(100) = 10,000$$
$$\sigma_S = \sqrt{10,000} = 100$$

Thus

$$P(T < 7100) = P\left(Z < \frac{7,100-7,000}{100}\right)$$
$$= P(Z < 1) = .8413$$

11-51. $V(Z) = V(3X-Y-5) = V(3X-Y)$
$$= V\left(3X+(-Y)\right)$$
$$\underset{independence}{=} V(3X)+V(-Y)$$
$$= 3^2 V(X)+(-1)^2 V(Y)$$
$$= 9(1)+2 = 11$$

Note: Observe that the wrong answer which you would obtain if you mistakenly wrote $V(3X-Y) = V(3X)-V(Y)$ is choice C. This is a common careless mistake.

11-52. Let X be the time until failure for the first generator and Y the time until failure for the second generator. Then the total time that the generators produce electricity is $T = X+Y$. We must make the realistic physical assumption that two separate machines have independent lifetimes. Using this assumption,

$$V(X+Y) \underset{independence}{=} V(x)+V(Y)$$

Both X and Y are exponential with mean $1/\lambda = 10$. Thus for each random variable the variance is $1/\lambda^2 = 100$.

$$V(T) = 100+100 = 200$$

11-53. At the end of this problem, we will indicate a shortcut solution, but first we will look at the problem directly. We need to find $Cov(X,Y) = E(XY) - E(X)E(Y)$. We have the additional problem of finding the unknown constant k. We can find k by using the relationship

$$1 = \int_0^1\int_0^1 kxdydx = \int_0^1\left[kxy\Big|_0^1\right]dx = \int_0^1 kxdx = k\frac{x^2}{2}\Big|_0^1 = \frac{k}{2} \rightarrow k=2$$

In order to find $E(X)$ and $E(Y)$ we need the marginal densities $f_X(x)$ and $f_Y(y)$. On the interval $(0,1)$ we have

$$f_X(x) = \int_0^1 f(x,y)\,dy = \int_0^1 2x\,dy = 2xy\Big|_0^1 = 2x$$

$$f_Y(y) = \int_0^1 f(x,y)\,dx = \int_0^1 2x\,dx = x^2\Big|_0^1 = 1$$

At this point we can finish the problem without finding expected values.

$$f_X(x)f_Y(y) = 2x = f(x,y).$$

Thus X and Y are independent, and $Cov(X,Y) = 0$.

Note: There is a result that says that if $f(x,y)$ can be factored into a product of functions of x and y alone, so that $f(x,y) = g(x)h(y)$ and the domain on which f(x,y) is defined is a rectangle, then X and Y must be independent. That would give you the solution to this problem in one step. We have found that some of our students try to use this in cases where the domain of definition is not a rectangle and it does not work. Shortcuts are fine, if used correctly.

11-54. We need to find $Cov(X,Y) = E(XY) - E(X)E(Y)$, with no shortcuts. The domain of definition for the joint density is the triangle R pictured below.

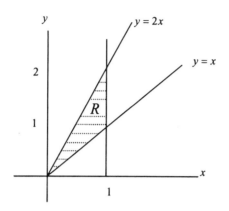

$E(XY) = \iint_R xyf(x,y) \ dy \ dx$

$= \frac{8}{3} \int_0^1 \int_x^{2x} x^2 y^2 \ dy \ dx$

$= \frac{8}{3} \int_0^1 \left[x^2 \frac{y^3}{3} \Big|_x^{2x} \right] dx = \frac{8}{3} \int_0^1 \left(\frac{7}{3} x^5 \right) dx = \frac{56}{9} \left(\frac{x^6}{6} \right) \Big|_0^1 = \frac{56}{54}$

$E(X) = \iint_R xf(x,y) \ dy \ dx$

$= \frac{8}{3} \int_0^1 \int_x^{2x} x^2 y \ dy \ dx$

$= \frac{8}{3} \int_0^1 \left[x^2 \frac{y^2}{2} \Big|_x^{2x} \right] dx = \frac{8}{3} \int_0^1 \left(\frac{3}{2} x^4 \right) dx = 4 \left(\frac{x^5}{5} \right) \Big|_0^1 = \frac{4}{5}$

$E(Y) = \iint_R yf(x,y) \ dy \ dx$

$= \frac{8}{3} \int_0^1 \int_x^{2x} xy^2 \ dy \ dx$

$= \frac{8}{3} \int_0^1 \left[x \frac{y^3}{3} \Big|_x^{2x} \right] dx = \frac{8}{3} \int_0^1 \left(\frac{7}{3} x^4 \right) dx = \frac{56}{9} \left(\frac{x^5}{5} \right) \Big|_0^1 = \frac{56}{45}$

$Cov(X,Y) = E(XY) - E(X)E(Y) = \frac{56}{54} - \frac{4}{5} \left(\frac{56}{45} \right) = .041$

11-55. In this problem we are given the marginal density for X and the conditional density for Y given x. Thus we can obtain the joint density, which is not given directly.

$$f_X(x) = \tfrac{1}{12},\ 0 < x < 12 \qquad f(y\,|\,x) = \tfrac{1}{x}\ 0 < y < x$$

$$f(x,y) = \tfrac{1}{12x},\ \ 0 < x < 12 \text{ and } 0 < y < x$$

We will find $Cov(X,Y) = E(XY) - E(X)E(Y)$, with no short-cuts. The domain of definition for the joint density is the triangle R pictured below.

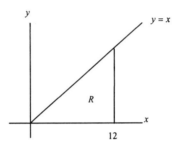

Since X is uniform on $(0,12)$, $E(X) = 6$. The other two expectations we need here will require some integration.

$$E(XY) = \iint_R xyf(x,y)\ dydx$$
$$= \int_0^{12} \int_0^x \tfrac{y}{12}\ dydx$$
$$= \int_0^{12}\left[\tfrac{y^2}{24}\Big|_0^x\right]dx = \int_0^{12}\left(\tfrac{x^2}{24}\right)dx = \left(\tfrac{x^3}{72}\right)\Big|_0^{12} = 24$$

$$E(Y) = \iint_R yf(x,y)\ dydx$$
$$= \int_0^{12} \int_0^x \tfrac{y}{12x}\ dydx$$
$$= \int_0^{12}\left[\tfrac{y^2}{24x}\Big|_0^x\right]dx = \int_0^{12}\left(\tfrac{x}{24}\right)dx = \left(\tfrac{x^2}{48}\right)\Big|_0^{12} = 3$$

$$Cov(X,Y) = E(XY) - E(X)E(Y) = 24 - 6(3) = 6$$

11-56. We will use the derivatives of the moment generating function to find the first two moments and thus obtain

$$V(X) = E(X^2) - E(X)^2.$$

First we rewrite the moment generating function and take derivatives.

$$M_X(t) = (1 - 2500t)^{-4}$$

$$M_X'(t) = -4(1 - 2500t)^{-5}(-2500) = 10,000(1 - 2500t)^{-5}$$

$$M_X''(t) = -50,000(1 - 2500t)^{-6}(-2500)$$
$$= 125,000,000(1 - 2500t)^{-6}$$

Then we evaluate the derivatives at $t = 0$ to obtain the moments and the variance.

$$M_X'(0) = 10,000 \qquad\qquad M_X''(0) = 125,000,000$$

$$V(X) = E(X^2) - E(X)^2$$
$$= 125,000,000 - 10,000^2 = 25,000,00$$
$$\sigma_X = \sqrt{V(X)} = \sqrt{25,000,000} = 5,000$$

11-57. Recall that $E(X^3) = M_X'''(0)$. First we will find $M_X(t)$. Note that $X = J + K + L$, where the summands are independent. Thus

$$M_X(t) = M_{J+K+L}(t)$$
$$= M_J(t)M_K(t)M_L(t)$$
$$= (1 - 2t)^{-3}(1 - 2t)^{-2.5}(1 - 2t)^{-4.5}$$
$$= (1 - 2t)^{-10}$$

$$M_X'(t) = -10(1 - 2t)^{-11}(-2) = 20(1 - 2t)^{-11}$$

$$M_X''(t) = -220(1 - 2t)^{-12}(-2) = 440(1 - 2t)^{-12}$$

$$M_X'''(t) = -12(440)(1 - 2t)^{-13}(-2) = 10,560(1 - 2t)^{-13}$$

$$E(X^3) = M_X'''(0) = 10,560$$

11-58. After revisions the total benefit is $X+100+1.1Y$. The required variance is

$$\begin{aligned}
V(X+100+1.1Y) &= V(X+1.1Y) \\
&= V(X)+V(1.1Y)+2Cov(X,1.1Y) \\
&= V(X)+1.1^2 V(Y)+2(1.1)Cov(X,Y) \\
&= 5,000+1.21(10,000)+2.2Cov(X,Y)
\end{aligned}$$

At this point we see that we need to find $Cov(X,Y)$. Note that we know $V(X)$, $V(Y)$ and $V(X+Y)$. Thus we have

$$V(X+Y) = V(X)+V(Y)+2Cov(X,Y)$$
$$17,000 = 5,000+10,000+2Cov(X,Y)$$

$$Cov(X,Y) = 1,000$$
$$\begin{aligned}
V(X+100+1.1Y) &= 5,000+1.21(10,000)+2.2(1,000) \\
&= 19,300
\end{aligned}$$

11-59. Since $C_2 = X+1.2Y$, we can put everything in terms of X and Y.

$$\begin{aligned}
Cov(C_1,C_2) &= Cov(X+Y,X+1.2Y) \\
&= Cov(X,X)+Cov(X,1.2Y) \\
&\quad + Cov(Y,X)+Cov(Y,1.2Y) \\
&= V(X)+1.2Cov(X,Y) \\
&\quad + Cov(X,Y)+1.2Cov(Y,Y) \\
&= V(X)+2.2Cov(X,Y)+1.2V(Y)
\end{aligned}$$

The given information must be used to find the variances and covariances above.

$$V(X) = E(X^2)-E(X)^2 = 27.4-5^2 = 2.4$$
$$V(Y) = E(Y^2)-E(Y)^2 = 51.4-7^2 = 2.4$$
$$V(X+Y) = V(X)+V(Y)+2Cov(X,Y)$$
$$8 = 2.4+2.4+2Cov(X,Y)$$
$$Cov(X,Y) = 1.6$$

Now we have the required information.

$$\begin{aligned}
Cov(C_1,C_2) &= V(X)+2.2Cov(X,Y)+1.2V(Y) \\
&= 2.4+2.2(1.6)+1.2(2.4) = 8.80
\end{aligned}$$

11-60. Let X_i be the claim amount on policy $i, i = 1,...,25$. The normal
random variables X_i are iid with mean $\mu = 19,400$ and variance
$\sigma^2 = 5000^2$. The average of 25 randomly selected claims is

$$\bar{X} = \frac{S}{25} = \frac{X_1 + \cdots + X_{25}}{25}.$$

$\bar{X}$ is normal with μ and variance $\frac{\sigma^2}{n}$.

$$E(\bar{X}) = \mu = 19,400$$
$$V(\bar{X}) = \frac{\sigma^2}{25} = \frac{5000^2}{25} = 1000^2$$
$$\sigma_{\bar{X}} = \sqrt{1000^2} = 1000$$

Thus

$$P(20,000 < \bar{X}) = P\left(\frac{20,000 - 19,400}{1,000} < Z\right)$$
$$= P(.6 < Z) = .2743$$

11-61. Let X_i be the lifetime of light bulb $i, i = 1,...,n$. The normal
random variables X_i are iid with mean $\mu = 3$ and variance
$\sigma^2 = 1$. The total lifetime of the succession of n bulbs is

$$S = X_1 + \cdots + X_n.$$

S is normal with

$$E(S) = \mu_s = 3n$$
$$V(S) = \sigma_s{}^2 = n(1) = n$$
$$\sigma_S = \sqrt{n}$$

We will find the unknown value of n using the requirement that
"the succession of light bulbs produces light for at least 40
months with probability at least 0.9772."

$$.9772 = P(S \geq 40)$$
$$= P\left(\frac{S - 3n}{\sqrt{n}} \geq \frac{40 - 3n}{\sqrt{n}}\right) = P\left(Z \geq \frac{40 - 3n}{\sqrt{n}}\right)$$

We can see from the Z tables that $P(Z \geq -2) = .9772$. Thus

$$\frac{40 - 3n}{\sqrt{n}} = -2 \rightarrow 3n - 2\sqrt{n} - 40 = 0$$

The last equation can be solved as a quadratic if we make the substitution $x = \sqrt{n}$.

$$3x^2 - 2x - 40 = 0$$

The positive root of this quadratic is $x = 4$. Thus $x = \sqrt{n} = 4$ and $n = 16$.

11-62. First we need to point out that the term "net premium" means the expected value of the amount paid by the insurance. Next we need to deal with the unknown value of K. Since the sum of the probabilities is one

$$1 = K + \frac{K}{2} + \frac{K}{3} + \frac{K}{4} + \frac{K}{5} = K\frac{137}{60} \rightarrow K = \frac{60}{137}.$$

The next table shows the loss N, the probability of each loss amount and the corresponding amount paid X after the deductible of 2.

Loss n	1	2	3	4	5
$P(N=n)$	$\frac{60}{137}$	$\frac{30}{137}$	$\frac{20}{137}$	$\frac{15}{137}$	$\frac{12}{137}$
Amount paid	0	0	1	2	3

The probabilities above are probabilities of claim amount and amount paid <u>given that a loss has occurred</u>. Thus

$$E(Amount\ Paid\,|\,Loss) = \frac{60}{137}(0) + \frac{30}{137}(0)$$
$$+ \frac{20}{137}(1) + \frac{15}{137}(2) + \frac{12}{137}(3)$$
$$= \frac{86}{137}$$

If there is not loss, the amount paid is 0. Thus

$E(Amount\ Paid)$
$= E(Amount\ Paid\,|\,Loss)P(Loss)$
$\qquad + E(Amount\ Paid\,|\,No\ Loss)P(No\ Loss)$
$= \frac{86}{137}(.05) + 0(.95) = .03139$

11-63. There are three possible cases here. Amounts are expressed in thousands.

  (a) No damage. Then $P(No\ Damage) = 1-.04-.02 = .94$ and $E(Amount\ Paid\,|\,No\ Damage) = 0$.

  (b) Full Damage. Then $P(Total\ Loss) = .02$ and $E(Amount\ Paid\,|\,Total\ Loss) = 15-1 = 14$

  (c) Partial Damage. Then $P(Partial\ Damage) = .04$, and we need to integrate to find the expected amount paid.

$$E(Amount\ Paid\,|\,Partial\ Damage)$$
$$= \int_1^{15} (x-1)f(x)dx$$
$$= .5003 \int_1^{15} (x-1)e^{-x/2}\,dx$$
$$= 1.2049$$

Then the expected amount paid in thousands is

$$.94(0)+.02(14)+.04(1.2049) = .328.$$

Multiplying by 1000, the expected amount paid is 328.

CHAPTER 12

The data in the table below is for the simulations in Exercises 12-1 and 12-2. The third column shows the number of coins player A has in 12-1 and the fourth shows which fund the employee in 12-2 is in at the end of each month.

Trial	Random Number	A has	Fund
Start		3	0
1	.57230	4	0
2	.85472	5	1
3	.37282	4	1
4	.77133	5	1
5	.20525	4	0
6	.82496	5	1
7	.52184	6	1
8	.49837	5	1
9	.76729	6	1
10	.50986	7	1
11	.02480	6	0
12	.99954	7	1
13	.81708	8	1
14	.90535		1
15	.76227		1
16	.78322		1
17	.00067		0
18	.24844		0
19	.14118		0
20	.47417		0

12-1. Player A wins a toss if the random number is in $[.5,1)$ and loses otherwise. The game ends when A has all 8 coins (he wins the game) or when he has 0 coins (he loses the game). From the table, A wins in 13 tosses.

12-2. If the employee is in Fund 0, he remains there if the random number is in $[0,.65)$ and switches otherwise. If he is in Fund 1, he switches if the random number is in $[0,.25)$ and stays there otherwise. From the table he is in Fund 1 thirteen times.

12-3. The waiting time X between accidents is exponentially distributed with $\lambda = 1$, so $F(x) = 1 - e^{-3x}$. To simulate waiting times, $x = F^{-1}(u) = -\ln\frac{1-u}{3}$. The following table simulates the waiting time between accidents and the cumulative time to the nth accident. From the table you count the number of accidents in the first few months.

Trial	Random Number	$F^{-1}(u)$ Waiting Time	Total Time
1	0.57230	0.28311	0.28311
2	0.85472	0.64303	0.92614
3	0.37282	0.15551	1.08165
4	0.77133	0.49183	1.57347
5	0.20525	0.07658	1.65005
6	0.82496	0.58091	2.23096
7	0.52184	0.24594	2.47690
8	0.49837	0.22996	2.70686
9	0.76729	0.48599	3.19285
10	0.50986	0.23769	3.43054
11	0.02480	0.00837	3.43891
12	0.99954	2.56143	6.00034
13	0.81708	0.56624	6.56657
14	0.90535	0.78586	7.35243
15	0.76227	0.47887	7.83130
16	0.78322	0.50962	8.34093
17	0.00067	0.00022	8.34115
18	0.24844	0.09520	8.43635
19	0.14118	0.05073	8.48708
20	0.47417	0.21426	8.70134

12-4. (a) $\mathbf{p}^{(1)} = \mathbf{p}^{(0)}\mathbf{P} = \begin{bmatrix} .50, & .50 \end{bmatrix} \begin{bmatrix} .65 & .35 \\ .25 & .75 \end{bmatrix} = \begin{bmatrix} .45, & .55 \end{bmatrix}$

   (b) $\mathbf{p}^{(2)} = \mathbf{p}^{(1)}\mathbf{P} = \begin{bmatrix} .45, & .55 \end{bmatrix} \begin{bmatrix} .65 & .35 \\ .25 & .75 \end{bmatrix} = \begin{bmatrix} .43, & .57 \end{bmatrix}$

12-5. (a) $\mathbf{p}^{(1)} = \mathbf{p}^{(0)}\mathbf{P} = \begin{bmatrix} .40, & .60 \end{bmatrix} \begin{bmatrix} .72 & .28 \\ .36 & .64 \end{bmatrix} = \begin{bmatrix} .504, & .496 \end{bmatrix}$

   (b) $\mathbf{p}^{(2)} = \mathbf{p}^{(1)}\mathbf{P} = \begin{bmatrix} .504, & .496 \end{bmatrix} \begin{bmatrix} .72 & .28 \\ .36 & .64 \end{bmatrix}$

   $= \begin{bmatrix} .54144, & .45856 \end{bmatrix}$

12-6. $\mathbf{p}^{(1)} = \mathbf{p}^{(0)}\mathbf{P} = [.30, .30, .40] \begin{bmatrix} .4 & .2 & .4 \\ .2 & .5 & .3 \\ .1 & .3 & .6 \end{bmatrix} = [.22, .33, .45]$

12-7. For this Markov process the transition matrix is

$$\mathbf{P} = \begin{bmatrix} .60 & .20 & .20 \\ .25 & .50 & .25 \\ .30 & .30 & .40 \end{bmatrix} \text{ and } \mathbf{p}^{(0)} = \begin{bmatrix} 1, & 0, & 0 \end{bmatrix}$$

$$\mathbf{p}^{(1)} = \mathbf{p}^{(0)}\mathbf{P} = \begin{bmatrix} .60, & .20, & .20 \end{bmatrix}$$

$$\mathbf{p}^{(2)} = \mathbf{p}^{(1)}\mathbf{P} = \begin{bmatrix} .60, & .20, & .20 \end{bmatrix} \begin{bmatrix} .60 & .20 & .20 \\ .25 & .50 & .25 \\ .30 & .30 & .40 \end{bmatrix}$$

$$= \begin{bmatrix} .47, & .28, & .25 \end{bmatrix}$$

12-8. To find the limiting distribution for the transition matrix in Exercise 12-4, we have to solve the following system of equations.

$$[x, \ y]\begin{bmatrix} .65 & .35 \\ .25 & .75 \end{bmatrix} = [x, \ y]$$

$$x + y = 1$$

or

$$.65x + .25y = x$$
$$.35x + .75y = y$$
$$x + y = 1$$

which can be rewritten as

$$-.35x + .25y = 0$$
$$.35x - .25y = 0$$
$$x + y = 1$$

The solution is $\left[\frac{5}{12}, \frac{7}{12}\right]$.

12-9. The limiting distribution for Exercise 12-5 is the solution of the following system of equations.

$$[x, \ y]\begin{bmatrix} .72 & .28 \\ .36 & .64 \end{bmatrix} = [x, \ y]$$

$$x + y = 1$$

This can be rewritten as

$$-.28x + .36y = 0$$
$$.28x - .36y = 0$$
$$x + y = 1$$

The solution is $\left[\frac{9}{16}, \frac{7}{16}\right]$.

12-10. The limiting distribution for Exercise 12-6 is the solution of the following system of equations.

$$\begin{bmatrix} x, & y, & z \end{bmatrix} \begin{bmatrix} .4 & .2 & .4 \\ .2 & .5 & .3 \\ .1 & .3 & .6 \end{bmatrix} = \begin{bmatrix} x, & y, & z \end{bmatrix}$$

$$x + y + z = 1$$

This can be rewritten as

$$
\begin{array}{rrrrcl}
-.6x & + .2y & + .1z & = & 0 \\
.2x & - .5y & + .3z & = & 0 \\
4x & + .3y & - .4z & = & 0 \\
x & + y & + z & = & 1
\end{array}
$$

The solution is $\left[\frac{11}{57}, \frac{20}{57}, \frac{26}{57} \right]$.

12-11. The limiting distribution for Exercise 12 –7 is the solution of the following system of equations.

$$\begin{bmatrix} x, & y, & z \end{bmatrix} \begin{bmatrix} .60 & .20 & .20 \\ .25 & .50 & .25 \\ .30 & .30 & .40 \end{bmatrix} = \begin{bmatrix} x, & y, & z \end{bmatrix}$$

$$x + y + z = 1$$

This can be rewritten as

$$
\begin{array}{rrrcl}
-.4x & + .25y & + .3z & = & 0 \\
.2x & - .5y & + .3z & = & 0 \\
.2x & + .25y & - .6z & = & 0 \\
x & + y & + z & = & 1
\end{array}
$$

The solution is $\left[\frac{15}{37}, \frac{12}{37}, \frac{10}{37} \right]$.

12-12. Let **P** be the transition matrix of a regular Markov process and let ℓ be its limiting distribution.

$$\ell\mathbf{P}^n = \ell\mathbf{P}^{n-1}\mathbf{P}$$

Taking the limit of both sides,

$$\lim_{n\to\infty}\mathbf{P}^n = \ell\lim_{n\to\infty}\mathbf{P}^{n-1}\mathbf{P}$$

$$\ell\mathbf{L} = (\ell\mathbf{L})\mathbf{P}$$

$$\ell = \ell\mathbf{P}^n$$

(Recall that for any vector $\mathbf{v}$, $\mathbf{vL} = \ell$.)

12-13. The transition matrix for the states for player A, after rewriting the matrix with the absorbing states first, is

$$\mathbf{P} = \begin{bmatrix} 1 & 0 & 0 & 0 \\ 0 & 1 & 0 & 0 \\ 2/3 & 0 & 0 & 1/3 \\ 0 & 1/3 & 2/3 & 0 \end{bmatrix}.$$

(a) $\mathbf{I}-\mathbf{Q} = \begin{bmatrix} 1 & -1/3 \\ -2/3 & 1 \end{bmatrix}$

$$(\mathbf{I}-\mathbf{Q})^{-1} = \begin{bmatrix} 9/7 & 3/7 \\ 6/7 & 9/7 \end{bmatrix} = \mathbf{N}$$

(b) $\mathbf{A} = \mathbf{NR} = \begin{bmatrix} 9/7 & 3/7 \\ 6/7 & 9/7 \end{bmatrix}\begin{bmatrix} 2/3 & 0 \\ 0 & 1/3 \end{bmatrix} = \begin{bmatrix} 6/7 & 1/7 \\ 4/7 & 3/7 \end{bmatrix}$

(c)   The probability that if player A starts in state 2 (2 coins) he ends in state 0 (he loses) is $a_{20} = \frac{4}{7}$. Recall that the rows in **A** refer to states 1 and 2 and the columns to states 0 and 3.

12-14. The transition matrix for the states for player A, after rewriting the matrix with the absorbing states first, is

$$\mathbf{P} = \begin{bmatrix} 1 & 0 & 0 & 0 & 0 \\ 0 & 1 & 0 & 0 & 0 \\ 2/3 & 0 & 0 & 1/3 & 0 \\ 0 & 0 & 2/3 & 0 & 1/3 \\ 0 & 1/3 & 0 & 2/3 & 0 \end{bmatrix}.$$

(a) $$\mathbf{I} - \mathbf{Q} = \begin{bmatrix} 1 & -1/3 & 0 \\ -2/3 & 1 & -1/3 \\ 0 & -2/3 & 1 \end{bmatrix}$$

$$(\mathbf{I} - \mathbf{Q})^{-1} = \begin{bmatrix} 7/5 & 3/5 & 1/5 \\ 6/5 & 9/5 & 3/5 \\ 4/5 & 6/5 & 7/5 \end{bmatrix} = \mathbf{N}$$

(b) $$\mathbf{A} = \mathbf{NR} = \begin{bmatrix} 7/5 & 3/5 & 1/5 \\ 6/5 & 9/5 & 3/5 \\ 4/5 & 6/5 & 7/5 \end{bmatrix} \begin{bmatrix} 2/3 & 0 \\ 0 & 0 \\ 0 & 1/3 \end{bmatrix}$$

$$= \begin{bmatrix} 14/15 & 1/15 \\ 4/5 & 1/5 \\ 8/15 & 7/15 \end{bmatrix}$$

(c) The probability that if player A starts in state 2 (2 coins) he will end in state 0 (he loses) is $a_{20} = \frac{4}{5}$.